WINTER IS COMING

Symbols and Hidden Meanings in A Game of Thrones

VALERIE ESTELLE FRANKEL

Thought Catalog Books
Brooklyn, NY

 Published by Thought Catalog Books, a division of The Thought & Expression Co., Williamsburg, Brooklyn. For general information and submissions: manuscripts@thoughtcatalog.com.

First edition, 2013
ISBN 978-0692591598
10 9 8 7 6 5 4 3 2 1

Founded in 2010, Thought Catalog is a website and imprint dedicated to your ideas and stories. We publish fiction and non-fiction from emerging and established writers across all genres.

Cover image by © iStockPhoto.com / Mlenny Photography
Cover design by www.athleticsnyc.com

CONTENTS

INTRODUCTION

For those who adore epic fantasy, *Game of Thrones* is riding hard on the heels of *Lord of the Rings.* Fans admiringly describe the complexity of the world, crammed with details from medieval Europe as armored heroes ride through magnificent ruins and ancient castles. Many consider *A Game of Thrones* more realistic than most fantasy, as many characters suffer serious injuries and die, unlike the gentler epics where a happy ending comes to everyone.

This book seeks to provide a deeper look into the series for fans. Who is Jon's mother and how can we tell? What is the source of Bran's magic? Or the Night's Watch's secret mission? Many have noticed that Westeros is medieval England, with a few visits from Dothraki Mongols, Eastern spice traders, and Celtic tree worshippers. But a deeper look reveals more specific reflections from our world as Zoroastrian Magi infiltrate Westeros, whose kings are reenacting the War of the Roses.

The books contain many prophecies that hint

tantalizingly at where characters will end, while the larger history of Westeros offers echoes between its past and future. Of course, Martin himself has dropped intriguing tidbits in posts and interviews. As all these elements mix, they highlight the real conflict of the series—that which is to come, or the prince who is promised, who will battle with ice and fire.

Spoilers are basically avoided; a few mentions are made of characters introduced or still living in the fifth book, but there are no mentions of significant deaths, marriages, etc. beyond season three of the show. Much on how the epic will end is speculation, some of which was set up as early as Old Nan's tales in the first episode.

George R.R. Martin, the books' author, is heavily involved on the show, which, though streamlined, is word-for-word accurate to the book in most scenes. Along with writing an episode each season and aiding with casting and set decisions, he remains close with the actors and writers. He notes:

> I talk constantly with David and Dan the executive producers and show runners. They've done an amazing job and stayed very faithful to the story. There've been some changes, but that's inevitable on a project like this. It's been a great ride so far and I hope it will continue for many years to come.[1]

1. John Birmingham, "A Conversation with Game of Thrones Author George RR Martin," *The Sydney Morning Herald.* Aug 1, 2011.

Thus, many of the revelations, prophecies, and subplots of the book series may be considered important to the television show. These are explored here, in the spirit of providing deeper insight into characters' motivations and possible destinies. Material in the book series is reasonably canon for the television show, providing background on the characters and their motivations. In the end, they aren't just fighting for the Iron Throne, but to preserve their entire world from the coming darkness. Let's learn how.

PART 1.

PUZZLE PIECES FITTED TOGETHER

CHAPTER 1.

YOU KNOW NOTHING, JON SNOW: THE REAL CONFLICT OF FIRE AND ICE

Game of Thrones has an awful lot of conflicts. However, none of the characters are managing to put the pieces together: The books are called *The Song of Ice and Fire.* Ice VERSUS Fire might be more accurate. A few things are clear (barring further revelations): The White Walkers are the real threat. Daenerys Targaryen is "meant" by her birth to destroy them with her fire and dragons as the realm's true protector. And she'll probably make it back home before it's completely desolated.

Tyrion notes: "The Seven Kingdoms will never be more ripe for conquest than they are right now. A boy king sits the Iron Throne. The north is in chaos, the Riverlands a devastation, a rebel [Stannis] holds Storm's End and Dragonstone. When winter comes, the realm will starve"

(V.281). Robb was warned that marching away from the Wall was the wrong way, and the Wall's commanders keep asking the south for aid. However, none comes. Each battle wastes more fighters, leaves more crops trampled into the ground. As Ned Stark warned from the beginning, Winter is Coming… and those who don't starve will be killed by the Others.

However, the characters are all ignoring this to kill each other, wasting entire armies that they already need in order to take a castle for an episode or two, destroy resources, and move on. They use the wildfire, dragons, and men only to attack one another. Now at last, winter is coming. And they may all be doomed.

WINTER IS COMING

Many of Old Nan's stories detail a world of long ago, with an endless winter and the terrible Others not seen in a thousand years. It seems clear that these evil forces are returning, and the heroes will need to fight them much as they did once before. Old Nan explains to Bran in the first episode:

> Oh, my sweet summer child. What do you know about fear? Fear is for the winter when the snows fall a hundred feet deep. Fear is for the long nights when the sun hides for *years*, and children are born and live and die, all in darkness. That is the time for

> fear, my little lord; when the white walkers move through the woods. Thousands of years ago there came a night that lasted a generation. Kings froze to death in their castles, same as the shepherds in their huts, and women smothered their babies rather than see them starve, and wept and felt their tears *freeze* on their cheeks. So is this the sort of story that you like? In that darkness the white walkers came for the first time. They swept through cities and kingdoms, riding their dead horses, hunting with their packs of pale spiders big as hounds.

Once more, winter is coming... and it seems the evil was defeated before but... how?

- In the book, after a nearly-identical speech, Old Nan tries to entertain Bran with a story about the Others: Thousands of years ago, a night lasted a generation, in the heart of winter. The Others came during that winter, and they hated "iron and fire and the touch of the sun" (I.240). Continuing the tale above, the last hero of the First Men set out to find the children of the forest, whose ancient magics could restore mankind's lost wisdom. He left with his sword, a dog, his horse, and twelve companions. When only he was left, the Others attacked... and then the tale is interrupted.

Certainly, our heroes need knowledge of how to fight the Others. Will Jon, with his knowledge of the Wildings, go on this quest? Or is Bran doing it for him? Is the dog significant—was this hero a shapechanging warg? Will the children of the forest, tiny mound-dwellers like the Celtic elves, tell our heroes how to defeat evil?

- When Bran and Rickon leave Maester Luwin in the Godswood at season two's end, six of them set out—exactly half of twelve, just as half of Bran is left to be a hero. Bran, Rickon, Hodor, Osha, Jojen, and Meera walk into the forest (in the book, these last two children were staying at Winterfell and escaped with the Stark boys).

If one adds the people, from guides to fellow travelers, the children find on the way North, the number reaches exactly twelve companions, at least for a night here and there. As Bran and his wolf travel steadily north, his story echoes the Last Hero's. He's even a descendent of the First Men, as all Northmen are. On his hero-quest, it's clear that Bran will descend into the darkest place all alone, as the Last Hero once did. There, he will confront the Other beyond the curtain, the one he has seen in his dreams. (See Bran's Dream in Chapter 5.)

- Describing the First Men, Jon says, "I think they were afraid. I think they came here [to Westeros] to get away from something. I don't think it worked" (2.5). Did the cold follow them from another place?

FIRE AND DOOM IN OLD VALYRIA

- The Targaryens with their dragons and magic came from Old Valyria, far to the east, source of lost secrets like Valyrian steel. The sky is always red above Valyria, and those who look on that land are doomed. Around it lays the cursed smoking sea. Thousands of years ago, every hill for five hundred miles exploded, filling the sky with fire and killing even the dragons. "Red clouds rained down dragonglass and the black blood of demons" (V.446). What happened? How did the Valyrians, with their dragons and magic, destroy their own world and cause their volcanoes to erupt?

In the present day, the greatest kingdoms of the western world are threatened by an invasion of ice-based creatures and an endless winter. One civilization was destroyed by fire, and the next will be destroyed by ice—all part of some grand cycle that we don't yet understand.

- In an interview, Martin answered why his saga is called *Ice and Fire,* saying that the Wall and the dragons were "the obvious thing but yes, there's more." He noted:

> People say I was influenced by Robert Ford's poem [clearly, Robert *Frost*'s poem is meant], and of course I was, I mean… Fire is love, fire is passion, fire is sexual ardor and all of these things. Ice is

betrayal, ice is revenge, ice is... you know, that kind of cold inhumanity and all that stuff is being played out in the books.[1]

> **Fire and Ice**
> by Robert Frost, 1920
>
> Some say the world will end in fire,
> Some say in ice.
> From what I've tasted of desire
> I hold with those who favor fire.
> But if it had to perish twice,
> I think I know enough of hate
> To say that for destruction ice
> Is also great
> And would suffice.[2]

The short poem links fire with desire and greed (a possible cause of the Doom of Valyria), while ice is equated with hatred—surely, even if the Others are not evil, their human adversaries are filled with hate and fear towards them. An instant, fiery explosion is said to destroy the world first, followed soon by a slow, icy death. The characters of Martin's saga are facing the latter.

- Six hundred years ago, Hardhome exploded north of the Wall. The "screaming caves" nearby seem to be "haunted by ghouls and demons and burning ghosts" (V.522). Was it the

1. "A Very Long Interview with George R.R. Martin," *Oh No They Didn't.com*, Oct 10 2012. http://ohnotheydidnt.livejournal.com/72570529.html
2. Robert Frost, "Fire and Ice," PoemHunter.com, 2003. http://www.poemhunter.com/poem/fire-and-ice.

same kind of volcanic explosion that destroyed Valyria? Or monsters under the earth, like the fabled ice dragons? Or firewyrms described as "boring" through soil and stone, as one of Dany's dragons does (IV:321)? Is this a clue that events are repeating?

- Summerhall is another mysterious disaster, happening at the time of Prince Rhaegar's birth and costing him his great-grandfather. King Aegon V sought to create a hot enough fire to hatch the petrified dragon eggs, but instead burned down himself and several family members in an intense conflagration. Ser Barristan recalls Summerhall as an incident of "sorcery, fire, and grief" (V:875). Were the Valyrians attempting a similar experiment?

DAENERYS'S BIRTHRIGHT

Daenerys comes from the line of hereditary royalty who managed to unite the kingdoms and protect them all with the might of dragons. They've always interbred, probably to keep their amazing dragon magic strong. She is the heir to Westeros, in a way that none of the quarreling families can claim. Illyrio Moptis, who arranges Daenerys's wedding to Drogo, later tells Tyrion: "There is no peace in Westeros, no justice, no faith… and soon enough, no food. When men are starving and sick of fear, they look for a savior. […] A savior comes from across the sea to bind up the wounds of Westeros" (V:30).

With the Targaryens gone, many claimants all battle for the throne, all of them selfish and flawed… suggesting that only the rightful monarch, one linked to the land, will end the unceasing war for resources and restore the ancient birthright.

Further, Daenerys may be more than the one true queen—she and her dragon magic may be the only weapon against the coming winter.

- The High Septon prayed for seven days and nights in Oldtown and then anointed Aegon the Conqueror. "For the Crone had lifted up her lamp to show him what lay ahead." (IV.421). He saw a future in which Westeros would need Targaryen rule.
- Today, Archmaester Marwyn believes in the Targaryens. He lives in "the oldest building at the Citadel," the Ravenry, where flocks of ravens perch among an ancient but still-living Godswood (IV.680). Perhaps just as the new gods told the Septon to trust in the Targaryens, the old gods offer the same message.

DAENERYS'S TRUE POWER

- Rhaegar as well as Prince Daeron (from Martin's short story "The Hedge Knight") and Daenerys have prophetic dreams, like the Starks. Like the Starks, Daenerys has raised her animals, sigil of her house, from babies. She may share the Stark gift for animal transformation, which has remained a secret only because her family has lacked the training. The direwolves have not been seen in Westeros for centuries, much like the dragons—both appear figures of prophecy, come to aid the chosen ones in the battle to come.
- Aerion the Monstrous (who's mentioned gleefully by Joffrey) died drinking a cup of wildfire, believing it would transform him into a dragon. Though he was mad, perhaps he'd read or dreamed some of the forgotten lore and knew the truth: the Targaryens' bond with dragons may be a warg bond, indicating they can ride in the minds of animals as the Starks can. He also saw wildfire as a substitute for dragonfire,
- Many fans are struck by mad prince Viserys, who swears Daenerys will anger him and "wake the dragon." He's later revealed to be powerless, as Daenerys is the only true child of the dragon, resistant to fire and capable of hatching the eggs. However, Viserys' ramblings have

interesting echoes. Prince Aerion (from "The Hedge Knight") shares a mad cruel temperament with Viserys and Aerion the Monstrous. All three claim that they *are* the dragon—this is more than coincidence and likely more than madness—the gift of prophecy and the instinct to transform are warped within them but real and manifesting itself. Perhaps Daenerys will truly "wake the dragon" and transform, like Bran and his siblings, into her animal companion. In turn, this would mean the Stark children could ride inside the minds of dragons.

SWORDS

Of course, in every hero tale, the hero receives a magical sword. The problem in this series is that too many swords are mentioned, at least in the books:

- Red Priestess Melisandre's flaming sword Lightbringer was created in legend by tempering a sword in the blood of the hero's wife:

> To fight the darkness, Azor Ahai needed to forge a hero's sword. He labored for thirty days and thirty nights until it was done. However, when he went to temper it in water, the sword broke. He was not one to give up easily, so he started over. The second

> time he took fifty days and fifty nights to make the sword, even better than the first. To temper it this time, he captured a lion and drove the sword into its heart, but once more the steel shattered. The third time, with a heavy heart, for he knew beforehand what he must do to finish the blade, he worked for a hundred days and nights until it was finished. This time, he called for his wife, Nissa Nissa, and asked her to bare her breast. He drove his sword into her breast, her soul combining with the steel of the sword, creating Lightbringer. (II:115)

This echoes Daenerys's experiences at the end of season one—that only death can pay for powerful magic. The sacrifice of Drogo's horse, like the lion in the Lightbringer tale, is not enough. Similarly, the magic to end the Others' attack will have to come from blood and sacrifice as well as power.

The stories of Azor Ahai and that of the dragons' origin in the world both mention a crack in the moon, subtly tying them together. If the dragons are Daenerys's Lightbringer, then Daenerys sacrificing Drogo to create them may have already fulfilled the prophecy. More likely, it set the stage for a greater sacrifice to come. And for this, the foretold hero will need a magic sword, whoever he or she may be.

- Stannis's Lightbringer has an unknown origin—Melisandre brought it from the east, so it may be real, or it may be a decoy with no magic whatsoever. It may or may not be Valyrian steel.

- Jon has Longclaw, a gift from his commander and a sword of bear and wolf, appropriate for a warg. (There are rumors the Mormonts are bear-wargs, though nothing has been proven.)
- One possibility for Lightbringer is the sword Oathkeeper, which a greedy Tywin forges from Ned Stark's sword Ice into a new red Lannister sword, blending ice and fire. It's strangely smoke-stained, and has already killed Ned Stark—a serious sacrifice for the Stark children, but since none of them chose it (despite Sansa's tiny betrayal), this loss likely foreshadows another greater sacrifice to come. Given eventually to Brienne, it might easily pass to a Stark and become the Oathkeeper of Daenerys and her allies, protecting Westeros. Its brother, given to Joffrey and named Widow's Wail, has a similar potential. If three swords are needed, for the three-headed dragon of Daenerys and her partners, this pair could both be needed.
- Another Targaryen sword is Dark Sister, blade of the Targaryen kings' bastard and spymaster Bloodraven, fate unknown. Arya specifically mentions it while serving as Tywin's page on the show, foreshadowing its importance. It may

be in the North with Bloodraven, and so pass to a Stark.

- If Tyrion Lannister is our hero and needs a sword, he knows where to find Widow's Wail in King's Landing. Another possibility for him or anyone is Brightroar, the ancestral sword of House Lannister. This name of course suggests the roar of flames as well as lions. It was lost in Valyria long ago (III: 359). If Tyrion discovers his ancestral sword, he may even prove to his family that he's a real Lannister.
- There are other magical swords: Ser Arthur Dayne's fabled Dawn glows with a white light and was carved from a meteor (echoing the red comet!). It famously passes only to one who's worthy, echoing the Lightbringer legend. With the metaphor of morning ending the long night, it may have a part to play—Maester Aemon even calls the upcoming endless winter the "war for the dawn" (III.884). The Sword of the Morning is a constellation, as is the Ice Dragon—ice and fire are enacting their battle in the heavens (III:355). However, Dawn's owner died battling Ned Stark at the Tower of Joy and Ned (allegedly) took it to the Dayne castle, where it sits unused. It may have a link with Jon, his biological family, or his tale. However, its lack of mention after book two suggests a lack of importance.

- Its counter is Blackfyre, Aegon the Conqueror's greatsword, "a fabled blade of Valyrian steel passed from king to king... until Aegon IV chose to bestow it on Daemon [his bastard son] instead of his legitimate son, Daeron... Some felt that the sword symbolized the monarchy, so the gift was the seed from which the Blackfyre Rebellions grew," Martin explains.[3] The Blackfyre children finally fled across the sea and founded the mercenary army known as the Golden Company. They attempted five more civil wars to take the throne, but all were unsuccessful. The fate of Blackfyre after the last of these battles, the War of the Ninepenny Kings, is unknown, but the Golden Company likely kept it. This sword may be closest to Dany geographically and would be fitting as the sword of her conqueror ancestor.
- The following conversation between Martin and a fan is intriguing, especially the final question:

Did the Targaryens own a family sword made of Valyrian steel, like Ice or Brightroar or Longclaw?

Several.

And if yes, what was it named and what happened to it – Rhaegar had it on the Trident, maybe?

3. "Correspondence with Fans," The Citadel: So Spake Martin, Aug 15 2001. http://www.westeros.org/Citadel/SSM/Category/C91/P90.

The most famous of them was named Blackfyre. It was long lost by Rhaegar's day, however.

Or, if you can't tell right now, will we find out about it in a later book?

Yes.[4]

- Along with the most obvious blades and mysterious Lightbringer, there are many swords of light and darkness, ice and fire. There's the dragonbone hilt dagger sent to hurt Bran and rumors of weirwood bows. Most lords have Valyrian steel swords. For instance, Sam's cruel father has the symbolically appropriate Heartsbane—how ironic if his son should need it to save Westeros as a great hero. Valyrian steel is rumored to kill the Others in ancient books of lore (V.100). Perhaps that's why the Houses have prized it so greatly.

MAGIC RETURNS

- Over the centuries, the White Walkers have faded until they're only legends. Likewise, over the centuries, the dragons diminished in size and power, and no one remembered their original importance. They are clearly tied together.
- As described in Martin's short stories, "The summers have been shorter since the last

4. Ibid.

dragon died, and the winters longer and crueler."[5] Are the Targaryens and their dragon powers holding back the winter merely by living and ruling?

- In the House of the Undying, Pyat Pree explains that the dragons have returned and brought magic back to the world. "It is strongest in their presence," he says, "and they are strongest in yours" (2:10). Daenerys apparently is magic incarnate. Though Pyat Pree doesn't know it, the White Walkers too have returned. Perhaps this magic freed them as well.
- Thoros of Myr (traveling with the Brotherhood without Banners in season three) is a red priest of R'hllor. He came to Westeros to convert Aerys Targaryen, after learning of his obsession with fire. Later, as he fought in the Riverlands, true powers awakened in him. Since Melisandre the Red Priestess is first seen in *A Clash of Kings*, a stranger to all in Westeros, her powers may be just as new, brought with the birth of dragons and the return of magic to the land. Like the Maesters, who try and fail to light dragonglass candles, the Maegi may have practiced the rituals with little or no power behind them, until recently. Also like the Maesters, the Maegi seem to know hidden lore

5. Martin, George R. R. "The Hedge Knight," Dreamsongs II (USA: Bantam Books, 2012), 607.

about magic and the ancient enemies in the North. R'hllor's religion may carry the truth of the upcoming battle against the Other, just as the Old Religion has true knowledge of Heart Trees.

- Everyone associates the red comet of *A Clash of Kings* with their own rise to power: King Joffrey sees Lannister red; Edmure Tully, Tully red. Brynden Tully, Aeron Greyjoy, and Osha all see an omen of war and bloodshed. Old Nan, whose ancient stories prove true, senses the coming of dragons. Certainly, the comet appears when Daenerys enters the fire and brings her dragons to life. But as it begins the second book, it also warns readers of the arrival of R'hllor, the god of fire, and his Red Priestess Melisandre. With her, magic arrives at Westeros. Her prophecies as she leads troops in the name of fire, against the mysterious Other, may be the best magic to battle the ice.
- Asshai-by-the-Shadow is the source of the world's cruelest sorcerers, who deal in fire magic and death magic: Melisandre, Mirri Maz Duur, Quaithe of the Shadow. (Mirri casts the death-spell that kills Dany's child, while Quaithe is the mysterious masked advisor living in Qarth).

To go to Asshai can be described as to "pass beneath the shadow." Though the "Shadow" has not been defined, it's the origin of the three dragon eggs. Asshai is also an exporter of dragonglass, and is the most likely to have the lost dragonlore. Since they still have magic, they may still have living dragons (which Bran Stark sees there in a vision).

All three of these sorcerous ladies seem to have a piece of the puzzle: Life must pay for life to hatch the dragons. The prince of prophecy must wield Lightbringer. And Quaithe's prophecies of the book may prove the most important:

> "To go north, you must go south. To reach the west, you must go east. To go forward you must go back, and to touch the light you must pass beneath the shadow."
>
> Asshai, Daenerys thought. She would have me go to Asshai. "Will the Asshai'i give me an army?" she demanded. "Will there be gold for me in Asshai? Will there be ships? What is there in Asshai that I will not find in Qarth?"
>
> "Truth," said the woman in the mask. And bowing, she faded back into the crowd. (II.426)

Apparently, to reach Westeros in the northwest, Daenerys must journey to Asshai in the southeast to find magic, dragonlore, or perhaps Lightbringer. It is a land of magic and lost knowledge, called "beside the shadow," indicating it has a knowledge of darkness but is not a source of darkness itself.

Another possibility is that one of the Maegi from Asshai, like Quaithe, will teach her what she needs. The "light" may be Lightbringer or enlightenment or goodness, and the shadow suggests the land near Asshai, or perhaps the shadow of danger and death. Melisandre births shadows and uses them to kill, but she comments that they need light to be cast—they represent magical strength, but not pure darkness.

Mirri Maz Duur is Daenerys's first magical mentor, Quaithe is the second. Though Melisandre has devoted herself to naming Stannis the prophesized prince, her lore is valuable and will apply to Daenerys, whether or not Melisandre becomes her third tutor. For indeed, "the dragon has three heads," and much of Daenerys's life is measured in threes.

OTHER WEAPONS

- The nastiest weapon anyone has is "wildfire" so vicious it can burn armies at a distance and won't go out... sort of a chemical substitute for dragons. The chief pyromancer on the show notes, "After the dragons died, wildfire was the key to Targaryen power... the substance is fire given form" (2.5). This suggests that the Targaryens who ordered wildfire made are the protectors of the realm, using the most powerful flames, whether dragonfire or wildfire, to destroy the Others. Neither was meant to be used for civil war.

- Lost in the North long ago, the fabled Horn of Joramun, or Horn of Winter, can allegedly bring down the Wall or awaken "giants from the earth" (II:276). Is it a tool of aid for the rangers or only a source of devastation? (If it's the horn Sam unearths, it was logically left by rangers for other rangers to find). Bran sees "the curtain of light at the end of the world," which might be shattered as easily as the Wall with the rangers' horn (I: 136-137). Is this its intended target? What giants is it meant to awaken? Could it wake dragons? Or the ice dragons of Nan's tales?
- At the other end of the world, in Old Valyria, Theon's uncle discovers a mysterious horn of fire called Dragonbinder that's fabled to control dragons. Black with red gold andValyrian steel, it feels warm to the touch. (Maester Aemon is suspicious of Stannis's Lightbringer specifically because it doesn't feel warm.) Its inscription of "*Blood for Fire, Fire for Blood*" matches the Targaryen motto, "Fire and Blood" and also the concept that life must pay for magic.
- This introduces odd paralleling: one horn can bring down the Wall and the other controls dragons? What if the Horn of Winter could bring down the Wall *by awaking the dragons, wyrm, or ice dragon buried beneath it?*

- By contrast, what if the other horn can control dragons, but it or many dragon horns were used to bring about the Doom of Valyria, blowing so hard they exploded the volcanoes? Could this also be what happened at Hardhome? Or Summerhall?
- What if the two horns are blown together? And is this how the series will end, with the world destroyed in ice and fire?

DRAGONGLASS

- Dragonglass can slay the corpselike wights. Many speculate that it's created by dragons. Whether or not this is true, it is clearly associated with them. Dragon fire was used to create "dragonsteel," Valyrian steel apparently. Clearly dragons and their fire are the best weapon to destroy the evil.
- On the show, dragonglass is positively identified as obsidian, volcanic glass. Old Valyria, filled with dragons, Valyrian steel, magic, and other lost secrets, was destroyed in the Doom of Valyria, a great explosion of a volcano chain. Are volcanoes the source of fire magic in the world?
- The rangers once knew dragonglass could defend them, as shown by the small stockpile

someone buried in the north, which Sam discovers at the Fist of the First Men. A small horn is also apparent in the box. The rangers also once worked closely with the Targaryens, who visited them and granted them lands and honors. Perhaps the dragon riders advised them to use dragonglass in battle.

- It's said Dragonstone Isle has a stockpile of dragonglass, left from the Targaryens. For some reason, they colonized Dragonstone, but not Westeros before Old Valyria was destroyed —perhaps the single island had the volcanoes they needed. "Odd, that,"Tyrion the scholar thinks. "Dragonstone is no more than a rock. The wealth was farther west, but they had dragons. Surely they knew that it was there" (V:76). What made Dragonstone so terribly important?

Dragonstone may still hold its secrets. Martin comments, "If you look at how the citadel of Dragonstone was built and how in some of its structures the stone was shaped in some fashion with magic… yes, it's safe to say that there's something of Valyrian magic still present."[6]

- Tyrion scrutinizes the Targaryen dragon skulls and sees each is "black as onyx due to its high

6. "Interview in Barcelona." Asshai.com, July 28, 2012. http://www.westeros.org/Citadel/SSM/Entry/Asshai.com_Interview_in_Barcelona.

iron content." The teeth are "long, curving knives of black diamond" (I:121). Dany's eggs too "shimmered like polished metal" and are heavy as stone (I:104). Are dragonbones and dragon eggs the source of dragonglass? Or merely similar in makeup?

- The children of the forest used to give the Night's Watch a hundred dragonglass daggers each year—they supplied them and worshipped in the weirwoods (V:100). Clearly, the children of the forest knew much about combating the Others.
- "The world the Citadel is building has no place in it for sorcery or prophecy or glass candles, much less for dragons" (IV.683). Like many, the Maesters have become obsessed with a new age of politics rather than the older truths of the Wall. Yet, as Martin tells it, "Oldtown =is= old, thousands of years old as opposed to King's Landing, which is only three hundred. Until Aegon's coming, it was the major city of Westeros. The Hightowers are one of the oldest families in the Seven Kingdoms." [7] Perhaps they hold the missing knowledge our heroes need.
- In their Citadel, the Maesters test their students by having them light a dragonglass candle. All fail, perhaps because they're not the

7. "Correspondence with Fans," The Citadel: So Spake Martin, Aug May 27, 1999. http://www.westeros.org/Citadel/SSM/Category/C91/P240.

Chosen One or because until recently magic had faded from the world. "All Valyrian sorcery was rooted in blood or fire. The sorcerers of the Freehold could see across mountains, seas, and deserts with one of these glass candles. They could enter a man's dreams and give him visions, and speak to one another half a world apart, seated before their candles" (IV:682). We've seen the horrors the Maegi can inflict with their magic of blood and sacrifice of the innocent. The other source of magic in the world is that of fire, the nobler tool.

Quaithe tells Daenerys "the glass candles are burning" (V:152-153). This indicates the return of magic, since for centuries the Maesters couldn't make them light. With magic comes the dragons, the Others and all the rest. But there may be more—if the Others are vulnerable to obsidian, these candles may be a warning system to defend against them.

THE WALL

- Men of the Night's Watch have always guarded the Southern lands, not from wildings, but from White Walkers. The oath on the show leaves out one line from the books, possibly for time:

Night gathers, and now my watch begins. It shall

> not end until my death. I shall take no wife, hold no lands, father no children. I shall wear no crowns and win no glory. I shall live and die at my post. I am the sword in the darkness. I am the watcher on the walls. *I am the fire that burns against the cold, the light that brings the dawn, the horn that wakes the sleepers, the shield that guards the realms of men.* I pledge my life and honor to the Night's Watch, for this night and all the nights to come. (I:522)

While the horn part is literally true, the Watch is supposed to fight White Walkers with fire and light, though they've only just started remembering that. This may foreshadow that Jon will *hold* the sword in the darkness, Lightbringer, and bring the fire that will heal the world. Likewise, Sam's mysterious horn from the dragonglass cache may wake much more than sleeping men.

- The Wall itself has the ancient magic of the Wierwoods, allowing none but rangers to pass. Rangers are sworn to fight the Others, though their mission lapses as the Others vanish. Now that they've returned, the Wall's powers may be waking as well.
- Melisandre's magic is stronger at the Wall (V:411). Daenerys's dragons and the Stark shapeshifting may gain strength there as well. Certainly Jon is closer to his wolf and wolf magic than Arya, Rickon, or Robb, though the

pair's day-to day partnership and perilous conditions may be responsible.

- Former Night's Watch Ranger Mance Rayder has made himself King-Beyond-the-Wall and united all the wildings into a single army. It seems that when he saw White Walkers, he realized the time had come to form an alliance of fighters. Westeros must do the same… once they find a strong ruler.

FIRE AND ICE CHARACTERS

One assumes an alliance of fire and ice characters will be needed to stop the war. Many believe Dany's three dragonriders will mix these characteristics, with perhaps northern Jon, dragon-riding Daenerys, and a child of south and north combined, like Bran. All the Stark children, raised at Winterfell, come from a red-haired mother from warmer climate. Robb, Sansa, Bran, and Rickon share her red hair and blue eyes. They also bridge the Old Religion and the New, the long Summer and coming Winter.

Other ice and fire symbolism:

- Wierwood trees are white with red leaves. Jon thinks that Ghost with his white fur and red eyes has similar coloring (V:466). These colors suggest a balance between the elements.

- The Lannister-Stark conflict that could be said to have begun the war is fought between the icy gray and white bannered north and the red and gold bannered south. Proposed matches from Sansa and Joffrey to Sansa and Tyrion echo this conflict.
- R'hllor is the god of fire and light; his devilish counterpart is a spirit of cold and darkness.
- Most of the Targaryen swords (above) are swords of either ice or fire.
- Gilly's son and foster-son. Jon comments, "You saved your own boy from the ice. Now save hers from the fire" (V:97).
- Griff (from the fifth book) has red hair dyed blue and wears the hide of a red wolf of Rhoyne. His eyes are "eye-blue, pale, cold" (V.120). "Young Griff," his foster son also dyes his hair blue, but claims a fiery parentage.

FIRE CHARACTERS

- Ygritte and Melissandre: "Ygritte had been kissed by fire; the red priestess *was* fire, and her hair was blood and flame." (V:52)
- Daenerys, born on an island of volcanoes and heir to the dragon magic.
- The Targaryens—possessors of ancient dragon

magic. Many have been obsessed with fire to the point of madness.

- Priests of R'hllor and anyone lit with the red priests' "inner fire."
- Princes and princesses of Dorne, land of hot deserts and hot tempers. Their sigil is the sun, and they are descended from Targaryens.
- The Lannisters, marked by gold and red. Their words, "Hear Me Roar," are fiery.

ICE CHARACTERS

- Wildings and Rangers, including Jon Snow
- The Starks, including siblings Ned, Benjen, and Lyanna, as well as cadet branches like the Karstarks.
- Mance Rayder, King Beyond the Wall

RELIGION, CUSTOMS, AND TELLING EXPRESSIONS

- "For the night is dark and full of terrors," chants the red priestess who insists on burning nonbelievers and worships fire as her savior. She says Stannis will save the world with fire. Though she is wrong in appointing Stannis the

Chosen One, the concept of fire as a savior seems accurate.

On the other hand, Melisandre, despite her superiority, interprets several of her visions wrongly. She may have misinterpreted the conflict as well. In many fantasy series, order defeats chaos or light defeats darkness only to discover the two need each other like Yin and Yang. Martin prides himself on having a saga of characters who feel justified in their aims, not ones who are wholly good or evil. After a fuller picture is revealed, fans come to sympathize with some of the cruelest. Likewise, it's clear the people of Westeros lack the full picture. The war of fire and ice may be one for balance, not eradication.

- "What is dead will never die," says the religionof the drowned god… vaguely echoing all these wights we're seeing up north. Some magic has the power to restore life, as seen through Lady Stoneheart and Coldhands. The red priests and priestesses have the power to return the dead to life, though these people do not become wights, but keep the priorities they had in life. Are these an anti-wight, made to combat the horrors of the north?
- "Let Theon your servant be born again from the sea, as you were. Bless him with salt, bless him with stone, bless him with steel." Salt, stone, and steel seem to be all the Ironmen have

surrounding them, so this may be a coincidence. But compare this to Lightbringer prophecy: "Azor Ahai shall be born again amidst smoke and *salt* to wake dragons out of *stone*." Two of the same elements, and the Lightbringer sword of Valyrian steel is the third. Both show a great hero returning from death, as Daenerys has done, as the drowned priests do, as a few other characters have done, as Drogo may do if the Maegi's prophecy is fulfilled. Do all religions know something the common folk have forgotten?

- "Valar Morghulis" (All Men Must Die) say the Faceless Men. Perhaps when they formed, they knew that the Others twist the lifecycle by reanimating the dead, and they must battle it. If so, their ties to Arya may prove useful. Martin says the Faceless Men have existed for "Thousands of years, if their traditions can be believed. Longer than Braavos itself" and that "their core organizing principle is religious."[8] They are eventually seen meddling in the Maesters' Citadel in Oldtown, possibly looking for books of lore.
- The Reeds' oath to Bran: "We swear it [fealty] by ice and fire." The Reeds pray to the old gods and have true dreams. With their knowledge of

8. Ibid.

prophecy, they may know that ice and fire are the most sacred things in the world.

CHAPTER 2.

JON'S MYSTERY MOTHER

IS JON NED STARK'S SON?

Though Ned identifies Jon's mother on the television show as "Wylla" when King Robert asks, the books give Jon a different mother in every book—Catelyn and Cersei think it's the Dornish Lady Ashara Dayne, sister to Ser Arthur Dayne of the Kingsguard, the Sword of the Morning and greatest warrior of his age. Catelyn asks Ned once.

> "Never ask me about Jon," he said, cold as ice. "He is my blood, and that is all you need to know. And now I will learn where you heard that name, my lady."
>
> She had pledged to obey; she told him; and from that day on, the whispering had stopped, and Ashara Dayne's name was never heard in Winterfell again. (I:65)

Ned and his friends killed Ser Arthur Dayne at the Tower of Joy under mysterious circumstances, and then took his fabled sword Dawn to Ashara Dayne at Castle Starfall. She in turn killed herself from grief. In the books, Wylla is Ashara's servant.

> "You told me once. Was it Merryl? You know the one I mean, your bastard's mother?"
>
> "Her name was Wylla," Ned replied with cool courtesy, "and I would sooner not speak of her."
>
> "Wylla, yes." The king grinned. "She must have been a rare wench if she could make Lord Eddard Stark forget his honor, even for an hour. You never told me what she looked like..."
>
> Ned's mouth tightened in anger. "Nor will I. Leave it be, Robert, for the love you say you bear me. I dishonored myself and I dishonored Catelyn, in the sight of gods and men." (I:111)

Note what is not said: Robert never actually met her, and Ned doesn't directly say Wylla was Jon's mother. Through shame or defensiveness, he asks Robert not to discuss it. Like King Robert, Ashara and Arthur's young nephew Edric Dayne thinks Wylla was the mother or at least the wetnurse (III: 494), but Lord Godric Borrell of the Three Sisters says Jon was the son of a fisherwoman from the Fingers—does Littlefinger know something about this? Ned refuses to tell anyone, from Catelyn to Jon when they ask, though he has muddled dreams of guilt and promises kept.

Robb and Jon, both honorable men, both have affairs when they shouldn't—Jon with the wilding Ygritte, though he has Night's Watch oaths, and Robb by wedding another when he's betrothed to a Frey girl. Both young men consider how their father, the soul of honor, had the one affair on Catelyn by succumbing to a momentary passion, and both young men discover how easy it is to do the same. For those who wonder how honorable Ned possibly could have cheated on his wife, here is an answer. Like his sons, he might have fallen for an inappropriate peasant or lady and had a desperate, illicit affair.

Jon, as stated repeatedly in the book, has Stark coloring with grey eyes and brown hair and clearly resembles his father. (In the family, Arya shares this coloring and she resembles her aunt Lyanna.) So one parent must be a Stark at least.

However, if Wylla is the mother, why hide it? In fact, since Wylla has told everyone at Starfall the child is hers, she's hardly desperate to keep the secret. It only seems likely Ned would keep silent if the mother is someone else. (Also note, he doesn't lie to Catelyn, he refuses to discuss it with her, most likely so he won't have to lie.) If Lady Ashara Dayne was the mother… she was noble, and she's dead (as far as anyone knows). Her son wouldn't be in the succession, even of her own lands. Even if Jon is heir to the house's fabled sword, Dawn, this would only allow him to enter a test of "worthiness."

Ned "had lived his lies for fourteen years, yet they still haunted him at night [Jon is fourteen in the first book]" (I:115). "The deceit made him feel soiled. *The lies we tell for love,* he thought. *May the gods forgive me*" (I:504). Jon's mother is a *secret,* but if Jon is not Ned's son, that is a *lie.* Is that the lie meant? Ned prays in the godswood that Jon and Robb will grow up "as brothers," suggesting (though not conclusively proving) that they're not. When Catelyn asks about Ashara Dayne, Ned says, "Never ask me about Jon...He is my blood, and that is all you need to know." My *blood,* not my *son?* Is Ned choosing his words particularly?

Clearly there's some mystery so dark Ned is sworn to silence, even against the inquiries of his king and his wife. Was this mother an escaped wilding of the North? A child of the wood? One of his older brother Brandon's illicit liaisons? Or, as many think, the son of Ned's sister Lyanna and Prince Rhaegar Targaryen?

TIMELINE

Prince Rhaegar, the mad king's heir, was obsessed with prophecy. He named his two children Rhaenys and Aegon after Aegon the Conqueror and his sister-wife, and craved a third child, a daughter, to complete this heroic triad. However, his wife Elia of Dorne had been rendered infertile after the second birth.

> Ned remembered the moment when all the smiles died, when Prince Rhaegar Targaryen urged his horse past his own wife, the Dornish princess Elia

> Martell, to lay the queen of beauty's laurel in Lyanna's lap. He could see it still: a crown of winter roses, as blue as frost. (I:631)

Rhaegar appointed Lyanna queen of love and beauty at the Harrenhal tournament, in front of everyone. When he ran away with Lyanna to the Tower of Joy in Dorne, Robert's Rebellion began. At the same tournament, according to Ser Barristan, Ashara had her own subplot:

> Even after all these years, Ser Barristan could still recall Ashara's smile, the sound of her laughter. He had only to close his eyes to see her, with her long dark hair tumbling about her shoulders and those haunting purple eyes. *Daenerys has the same eyes.* Sometimes when the queen looked at him, he felt as if he were looking at Ashara's daughter...
>
> But Ashara's daughter had been stillborn, and his fair lady had thrown herself from a tower soon after, mad with grief for the child she had lost, and perhaps for the man who had dishonored her at Harrenhal as well. She died never knowing that Ser Barristan had loved her.

Ser Barristan believes "Stark" was the father of Ashara's child—possibly Ned and possibly his brother Brandon.

This mention that Daenerys has Lady Ashara's eyes and Ashara had a stillborn *daughter* is intriguing. However, this appears to be another false clue—Ashara's stillborn child would have been about two years older than Daenerys and one year older than Jon.

Edric Dayne says that Ned Stark and Ashara fell in love at Harrenhal, but he wasn't there, so he's only quoting rumor (III 495). Meera Reed has heard a family legend that Ned and Ashara danced together at the tourney at Harrenhal: "The crannogman saw a maid with laughing purple eyes dance...with the quiet wolf...but only after the wild wolf [his older brother Brandon Stark] spoke to her on behalf of his brother too shy to leave his bench" (III. 281). The quiet wolf was probably Ned (though this is obscured at least a bit), and Ashara had striking purple eyes. But a dance, an affection, or even an affair a year before Jon's conception proves nothing.

Why keep the secret? To protect Edric, her living nephew from embarrassment? Or is there some deeper secret here? Ashara was the Targaryen queen's lady—did she smuggle the baby prince Aegon Targaryen to safety? Or hide him before the Lannisters murdered him? (Jon doesn't look Targaryen, so if Jon is Aegon, there was some major face swapping. It seems a stretch that some Faceless Man took the face from the dead Stark bastard Ashara possibly had a year before and gave it to Aegon/Jon so he could grow up in obscurity.)

Ned fought in the war during Jon's conception, ranging through the North and the Riverlands, but not as far south as King's Landing or Dorne. It's possible that Ashara and her maid Wylla journeyed north to see him, perhaps to resume

Ashara's affair from the tournament. In wartime, however, this seems unlikely and unsafe. Another possibility is his meeting with a wilding girl or someone completely unsuitable, even treasonous, but there have been no rumors of such a thing.

Prince Rhaegar "returned from the south" towards the end of the war (III: 418), where he had presumably been with Lyanna. He was killed in battle at the Trident. His wife, daughter, and (probably) infant son Aegon were killed in King's Landing—baby Aegon's corpse was unrecognizable, and there are rumors of his survival.

The Tournament happened before the war; the war lasted almost two years. Brandon died just before the war, and Ned inherited his brother's betrothed, Catelyn, along with Winterfell. The pair married a few months into the war, and then Ned left Catelyn (his wife but a near-stranger) pregnant with Robb and returned to battle. Robb is slightly older than Jon. Jon was born near the war's end within a month of Mad King Aerys' and baby Aegon's death. Lyanna died shortly after the war, and then Ashara Dayne killed herself. Jon was not born "more than one year" before Daenerys according to Martin—probably closer to eight or nine months or thereabouts. As such, he's born around Rhaegar's death.[1] Aegon Targaryen,

1. "Correspondence with Fans," The Citadel: So Spake Martin, July 30 1999. http://www.westeros.org/Citadel/SSM/Category/C91/P225.

Rhaegar and Elia's child, was killed at the same time as his grandfather, though the body was not identifiable as his. Baby Aegon was likely about a year older than Jon.

Following Robert's victory, Ned Stark traveled to the Tower of Joy, where Rhaegar had taken his sister Lyanna. Ned and his six companions battled Ser Arthur Dayne, Ser Oswell Whent, and Lord Commander Gerold Hightower of the Kingsguard there, and only Ned and his friend Howland Reed (father to Jojen and Meera) survived. Lyanna died in the tower, amid some amount of mystery (I:354-355). There was a fever, much blood, and a promise that drives Ned through all of the first book.

> He could still hear her at times. *Promise me,* she had cried, in a room that smelled of blood and roses. *Promise me, Ned.* The fever had taken her strength and her voice had been faint as a whisper, but when he gave his word, the fear had gone out of his sister's eyes. (I: 43)

Ned's dreams of this event are muddled and only offer further mysteries—What was the promise? Why were the Kingsguard there, with no (known) Targaryens present? Why was Ned fighting them after the war ended? To rescue Lyanna from those who kidnapped her for the prince to rape? To defend his sister's honor? To save her? Since Rhaegar was already dead, why would the Kingsguard stop Ned from taking his sister away?

Did the Kingsguard and Lyanna have different plans for her baby? Martin comments, "We will meet Howland Reed, but [not soon]…he knows just too much about the central mystery of the book."[2] Since Reed is the only one still living who was there at the Tower of Joy and Ned's subsequent trip to Dorne, from which he returned with Jon, Howland Reed will likely reveal the truth to our characters.

After Lyanna died in the Tower of Joy, Ned delivered Ser Arthur Dayne's miraculous sword Dawn to Lady Ashara Dayne at Starfall, who killed herself. Her motive for suicide is unclear – her brother's death? Or Ned's leaving her for Catelyn and taking their child? Ashara Dayne is described as striking, with dark hair and violet eyes. Did she and Ned have an affair? Was she already the mother of his brother Brandon's bastard? Or did she participate in a cover-up? Did Ned carry his sister Lyanna's baby to her and ask for her secrecy while her maid Wylla acted as wet-nurse?

Martin notes:

> Ashara Dayne was not nailed to the floor in Starfall, as some of the fans who write me seem to assume. …she was one of Princess Elia's lady companions in King's Landing, in the first few years after Elia married Rhaegar"[iii]

This gave her the opportunity to meet Brandon

2. "Correspondence with Fans," The Citadel: So Spake Martin, Nov 16 2000. http://www.westeros.org/Citadel/SSM/Entry/1261.

Stark, or possibly to aid the Targaryens smuggling a child or Lyanna to safety.

After all these events, Ned rode home with baby Jon. Certainly, many babies with mysterious parents and royal origins were born around this time, but surely the adults around Daenerys or Jon would have noticed the age discrepancy if a switch of some sort had been made…though the possibility exists of Ashara and "Stark" resuming the affair and having a second child later, adding another child to the puzzle. Ashara and Arthur's nephew and heir Edric Dayne, twelve years old in the third book, was born after these events and is clearly not Aegon Targaryen or a Stark.

IS JON BRANDON STARK'S SON?

Brandon was known for affairs, and there's the intriguing affair "Stark" had with Ashara Dayne. However, Brandon was killed too early to be Jon's father. Likewise, Benjen Stark spent the war in Winterfell and does not appear connected with these events.

If Brandon Stark had an affair while betrothed to Catelyn, Ned might claim the child, though doing so while *he* was married to Catelyn would be problematic—his having a bastard as Catelyn's unfaithful husband is more humiliating for her than her dead fiancé doing so. If Brandon *married* someone secretly, though, that legitimate child would actually be the heir to Winterfell, not Ned (Little Bran notes that the first son's son inherits before the second son.) If Ned needed to protect Winterfell from those who would attack a child lord, he might rule. But it seems unlikely the soul of honor would let Jon the secret heir go to the Wall and keep Winterfell for himself and his own sons. Further, if Jon is Brandon's son, there's really no reason to hide it.

IS JON LYANNA STARK AND RHAEGAR TARGARYEN'S SON?

The Targaryen connection would make sense, as Ned would protect a young Targaryen from Robert, who let young Aegon and his sister be slain and whose "hatred of the Targaryens was a madness in him" (I:112). And Ned, willing to die for honor, seems unlikely to have betrayed his new wife Catelyn, pregnant with his child… more likely, he valued his dying sister and her child above all—even that new wife's sensibilities. An honorable man doesn't cheat on his wife, but an honorable man protects his sister's child and keeps his oath to tell no one his parentage… even if this creates family discord. Lyanna's final words, "Promise me," haunt Ned through the first book. She lay dying surrounded by blood… unlikely for a fever, more plausible for childbirth. In turn, her suicide or murder makes the fever unlikely unless the wound went septic. And what promise was it, if not that Ned take her child?

Jon resembles his father *and Lyanna.* (In the book, all of Ned and Catelyn's children are red-haired like the Tullys except for Arya who resembles Ned. Lyanna is described as resembling Arya with the traditional Stark coloring.) This would also explain the Kingsguard's presence guarding Lyanna instead of fighting beside their prince at the Ruby Ford—they are sworn to protect the king and his family, so why else would they be at the Tower of Joy? Three fight with Rhaegar on the Trident, one (Jaime Lannister) defends the king himself plus Rhaegar's wife and children in the capitol. None guard the queen, Viserys, and unborn Daenerys. And three members of the Kingsguard, including the two most legendary, are guarding Rhaegar's girlfriend?

Daenerys's vision in the House of the Undying includes blue roses (Lyanna's favorite) blooming from an ice wall, a likely allusion to Lyanna's child at the Wall (II:515-516). It also parallels the book's legend of Bael the Bard and the blue rose, in which a Stark daughter is stolen from the family, only to give the House a son by her lover.

The blue rose image certainly repeats in Ned's memories, as Lyanna begs for his help. "He thought of the promises he made to Lyanna as she lay dying, and the price he'd paid to keep them" (I:380). One promise is to bury her at Winterfell, but that wouldn't have a heavy price. However, Catelyn's and Jon's lives have been made miserable because of the secret.

Another interesting parallel in Ned's thoughts may be a clue:

> He remembered Rhaegar's infant son, the red ruin of his skull, and the way the king had turned away, as he had turned away in Darry's audience hall not so long ago. He could still hear Sansa pleading, as Lyanna had pleaded once. (I:199)

Sansa pleaded for her pet's life, and Robert ignored her just as he let the Targaryen children die without mercy. These in Ned's mind are tied to Lyanna's plea—to protect another innocent from Robert's wrath. Robert had already sworn to eliminate the Targaryens, and smiled at the death of Rhaegar's other children. Only total secrecy would guarantee Jon's safety. Within a page of discussing Wylla with Robert, Ned's thoughts turn to the young Targaryen children and Lyanna both dying in the war.

> Ned thought, *If it came to that, the life of some child I did not know, against Robb and Sansa and Arya and Bran and Rickon, what would I do? Even more so, what would Catelyn do, if it were Jon's life, against the children of her body.* He did not know. He prayed he never would. (I:486)

This quote has a few intriguing teases: Ned lists his children but leaves out Jon. Perhaps not his child? He also fears that Catelyn cannot be trusted with Jon's life, because everyone has a price. This emphasizes why he's told *no one*—not Catelyn, not Jon, not his trusted friends. When he and Jon part, the men who ordered all Targaryens dead still live, and King Robert is visiting. There's still a need to keep the secret.

Likewise, Bran and Jon have intriguing dreams that there's an important secret about Jon in the crypts, where Lyanna is buried (see Jon's Dreams). Certainly, if he is their son, this would make him a child of ice and fire with Winterfell warg powers and dragon magic, the hero of prophecy. In his studies, did Rhaegar see prophecies pointing to such a child? If Jon is a Targaryen, he shares Daenerys's ancient magic and her destiny: A child of the forest said that "the prince that was promised would be born of their line," the line of Mad King Aerys and Rhaella (V:300-301).

Rhaegar believed in this destiny and insisted that he must have three children to mimic Aegon the Conqueror and his two sister-wives, that "there must be one more," since "the dragon has three heads." However, his wife was infertile afterward, and he may have tried to conceive a third child with Lyanna. This may have been rape, but naming it the "Tower of Joy" suggests love. Either way, he kept Lyanna close and they were indisputably lovers.

It should be noted that the Targaryens practiced

bigamy. Though this was basically in the distant past, Rhaegar considered his children to be Aegon the Conqueror and his sisters reborn, so he might have wed Lyanna secretly, repeating the cycle of Aegon and his double marriage. Naming his son and daughter after Aegon the Conqueror and his sister Rhaenys emphasizes this and also suggests he was awaiting a third child to name Visenya, and complete the pattern. As a bastard, Jon is not technically in the succession (though he would still be heir to Targaryen dragon magic, destiny, and prophecy). If he is a trueborn son, Jon would be in line after his older half-brother Aegon, if he is alive, and before Daenerys, his aunt and later in the succession. (It should also be noted that since the civil war called the Dance of the Dragons, females are specifically barred from the throne. Her son would inherit in her place.)

If Jon's parents were married, it once again seems unlikely Ned would let him go to the Wall if he knows Jon is the Targaryen heir. (On the other hand, Ned is loyal to Robert and wants peace in the realm, so he may be willing to sweep Jon's nebulous claim under the rug. The Targaryens were conquered, after all.) It's more likely Jon's parents were not married. Ned would believe that as a bastard, Jon might as well find safety and honor at the Wall, since he's not a trueborn heir.

Aegon the Conqueror reborn is certainly Daenerys, who with her three dragons will come from over the sea and conquer Westeros. To do this, she will likely need two male dragonriders as partners and (possibly) husbands. Bastard or no, if Jon is Rhaegar's son, he, like young Aegon Targaryen, is prophesized to be Daenerys's perfect mate. Martin comments only, "Jon's parentage will be revealed eventually," though we had little cause to doubt it. [3]

3. "Correspondence with Fans," The Citadel. So Spake Martin, Aug 15 2001. http://www.westeros.org/Citadel/SSM/Category/C91/P90.

PART 2.

BORN AGAIN AMIDST SMOKE AND SALT: EXPLORING PROPHECY

The book series offers several important prophecies that drive the narrative and point toward where the heroes are heading. In the House of the Undying on the show, Daenerys has an emotional meeting with her lost husband and son, but does not see the book's visions of the future or hear the prophecies that will drive her life. The reason for this, as Martin pointed out at the World Science Fiction and Fantasy Convention, is clear: The producers had no guarantee that the show would last until all the prophecies could be fulfilled, or for that matter, that minor threads, characters, and subplots wouldn't be cut for time. As such, they didn't wish to promise prophecies that might or might not be completed within the show. The book has more freedom, as Martin is certain of major events.

There are other sources of prophecy as well. Maegi appear to prophesize truly, although the Red Priestess has some embarrassing moments when she *sees* correctly but interprets wrong. For instance, she sees a girl in grey and assumes it's Arya Stark, but it isn't—many brown-haired girls can wear grey after all. Likewise, she appears to be correct about the hero with a flaming sword, but there's significant evidence that it won't be her chosen king, Stannis. Thoros of Myr, who travels among the Brotherhood without Banners, is a red priest from the same order.

Several characters such as Bran, Daenerys, and

occasionally Jon have prophetic dreams. These are given to them by their wolves or through the magical Targaryen birthright. (Jaime's dreams, by contrast, appear to be products of guilt rather than omens of the future). Martin has commented that all the Stark children have the wolf powers—for instance, little Rickon also dreams of his father's death and Arya slowly begins to communicate with her wolf. Sansa may have lost this potential with her own wolf's death in season one.

In the second book (or episode 3.2), Jojen Reed arrives to be Bran's friend and tutor. He too has true dreams. Many of these dream prophecies have already come true, and all of them indicate the events to come.

Of course, Martin notes that prophecies can still surprise people, warning that "Not all of them mean what they seem to mean..."

> Prophecies are, you know, a double edge sword. You have to handle them very carefully; I mean, they can add depth and interest to a book, but you don't want to be too literal or too easy... In the Wars of the Roses, that you mentioned, there was one Lord who had been prophesied he would die beneath the walls of a certain castle and he was superstitious at that sort of walls, so he never came anyway near that castle. He stayed thousands of leagues away from that particular castle because of the prophecy. However, he was killed in the first battle of St. Paul de Vence and when they found him dead he was outside of an inn whose sign was the picture of that castle! [Laughs] So you know?

> That's the way prophecies come true in unexpected ways. The more you try to avoid them, the more you are making them true, and I make a little fun with that.[1]

Many of the presented prophecies have come true—five of the seven books have been released after all. The more important prophecies (without significant spoilers) are presented in this chapter for fans who would like to explore their text and discover the shape of what is to come.

1. Ibid.

CHAPTER 3.

THE COMING OF THE CHOSEN ONE

[Mild book five spoilers of a new character and some revelations that may or may not be true]

> In the ancient books it's written that a warrior will draw a burning sword from the fire, and that sword shall be Lightbringer. Stannis Baratheon, warrior of light, your sword awaits you. (2.1)

With these words, Melisandre the Red Priestess calls Stannis to be the Chosen One and prophesized king. Melisandre also warns that the seas will freeze and "the dead shall rise in the North" (2.1). The time has come for a champion to heal the world. In the books, Melisandre goes into more detail:

> "When the red star bleeds and the darkness gathers, Azor Ahai shall be born again amidst smoke and salt to wake dragons out of stone."
>
> "There will come a day after a long summer when the stars bleed and the cold breath of darkness falls

> heavy on the world. In this dread hour a warrior shall draw from the fire a burning sword. And that sword shall be Lightbringer, the Red Sword of Heroes, and he who clasps it shall be Azor Ahai come again, and the darkness shall flee before him." (II:110)

However, there's a dark side to the prophecy:

> To fight the darkness, Azor Ahai needed to forge a hero's sword. He labored for thirty days and thirty nights until it was done. However, when he went to temper it in water, the sword broke. He was not one to give up easily, so he started over. The second time he took fifty days and fifty nights to make the sword, even better than the first. To temper it this time, he captured a lion and drove the sword into its heart, but once more the steel shattered. The third time, with a heavy heart, for he knew beforehand what he must do to finish the blade, he worked for a hundred days and nights until it was finished. This time, he called for his wife, Nissa Nissa, and asked her to bare her breast. He drove his sword into her breast, her soul combining with the steel of the sword, creating Lightbringer. (II:115)

Azor Ahai clearly must sacrifice his great love to become his world's champion. While characters like the Starks have lost loved ones, this was likely not a deliberate enough loss. Daenerys has more intentionally sacrificed her unborn child, but specifically to save her husband. The sacrifice brought forth the dragons, but also serves to show readers a great loss indeed is needed for great magic. The dragons may be Dany's Lightbringer, but since dragons and a sword are both mentioned in the prophecies, a sword of light will likely be needed as well. Melisandre and Stannis' schemes of burning unbelievers and royal captives is almost certainly not enough of a sacrifice, though Stannis does have an only child he might feel compelled to kill…

Waking dragons from stone is also interesting. Granted, Daenerys has hatched her dragons from stone eggs, but more may be coming. Many fans have wondered if the Targaryen home territory of Dragonstone with its stone dragon sculptures has actual dragons waiting to emerge. There are rumors of a dragon under the ice on the Wall. Bran (in a scene watched by his wolf Summer) may even have awoken a dragon as Winterfell burned. (See Bran as Chosen One)

Of course, the words are ambiguous. Targaryens are referred to as dragons, so a Targaryen might be resurrected or "brought forth from stone." Jon's Targaryen identity may have a clue waiting in Winterfell's stone crypts. Those infected with greyscale, like Stannis's daughter Shireen, are called "stonemen." (If a Targaryen or Targaryen heir is infected with greyscale, the prophecy could come true in that sense.) Greyscale petrifies and is "unclean" according to the wildings, so Shireen's sacrifice may be at hand.

Along with the prophecy of Azor Ahai, there's

also the Prince Who Was Promised, who may or may not be the same person: Prince Rhaegar, Daenerys's older brother and heir to the throne before his death, named his son Aegon after Aegon the Conqueror and added, "What better name for a king?" In the House of the Undying vision, he said, "He is the prince that was promised, and his is the song of ice and fire...The dragon must have three heads" (II.701). Though a three-headed dragon is the Targaryen crest, this last sentence is quoted later by Ser Jorah and Dany to suggest the dragonriding champion must have two partners... or even spouses. Daenerys' three dragons support this theory, as she mentions her ancestors only every rode a single dragon each. With three mounts, she needs three riders.

Based on Tyrion's and Quentyn Martell of Dorne's comments in the fifth book, a dragon is far more likely to accept a dragonrider with Targaryen blood. There's been no mention of Starks, Tullys, or Lannisters having Targaryen ancestors, and it's mentioned that great houses rarely intermarry, but it's quite possible. Cersei thinks the Targaryens possess "the blood of Old Valyria, the blood of dragons and gods" (IV:360). It may be truer than she knows.

Characters with Targaryen Blood

- Daenerys of course
- Baby Aegon, if he lives and is who he says

- The Golden Company: After the Blackfyre Rebellion failed, King Aegon IV's legitimized bastard Aegor Rivers, called "Bittersteel," fledWesteros with the surviving sons of the king's other bastard Daemon Blackfyre, and formed the greatest mercenary company in the world, out in the Free Cities.
- The Martells: Doran, Lord of Dorne, his three children, his brother Oberyn and his many bastard daughters the Sand Snakes.
- The Baratheons, their trueborn children (Shireen but not Joffrey), and Robert's numerous bastards—his acknowledged son Edric Storm is in Lys at last report, while the few others who survived Joffrey's purge are in Westeros.
- Bloodraven
- Maester Aemon
- Possibly Jon Snow (depending on his parentage)

Further, Melisandre is eager to sacrifice those with a king's blood, as she pronounces: "The Lord of Light cherishes the innocent. There is no sacrifice more precious. From his king's blood and his untainted fire, a dragon shall be born" (III: chapter 54). In this case, it's almost easier to name characters who *don't* have king's blood: The Starks, Greyjoys, and most other great houses were kings before Aegon the Conqueror (some Houses died out and others were advanced in their places, so not every great house fits this description). There's everyone who's named themselves kings in recent years, including Mance Rayder. And all the bastards once again. Melisandre seems eager for innocents in particular, though it's unclear which factors do in fact make the best sacrifice. Her insistence on sacrificing royal children echoes Azor Ahai's sacrifice of a lion—powerful-looking, but not the required sacrifice of the heart. Once again, she seems misguided in her approach.

Here, Melisandre links the three concepts: Azor Ahai, the prince who was promised, and the war against the Others:

> "Make no mistake, good sers and valiant brothers, the war we've come to fight is no petty squabble over lands and honors. Ours is a war for life itself, and should we fail the world dies with us."
>
> . . .
>
> All of them seemed surprised to hear Maester Aemon murmur, "It is the war for the dawn you speak of, my lady. But where is the prince that was promised?"
>
> "He stands before you," Melisandre declared, "though you do not have the eyes to see it. Stannis Baratheon is Azor Ahai come again, the warrior of fire." (III.884)

Maester Aemon seems to have read of this lore (perhaps in the Citadel where he was trained) and calls it the war for the dawn. Since Old Nan's description of the long winter included endless night, this makes sense. But who is this Chosen One meant to lead?

STANNIS AS CHOSEN ONE

Stannis fits somewhat. Melisandre the red priestess, of course, insists that it's him, although her agenda could be anything in the world, including the downfall of Stannis or all of Westeros.

He's sacrificed many, but the stone dragons in his castle at Dragonstone haven't awakened.

Stannis has an impressive flaming sword, but there's no evidence it's the real Lightbringer. Maester Aemon is skeptical because it remains cold. Further, the red priest Thoros of Myr who uses flaming swords as a tournament trick emphasizes this sword's likely illusion. Gendry reports: "He'd just dip some cheap sword in wildfire and set it alight. It was only an alchemist's trick" (III:308). One critic notes:

> To recreate Lightbringer, Stannis symbolically sacrifices idols of his old faith, the Seven, in a great bonfire, and then draws the blade out of the burning form of the Mother. However, Stannis does not seem to have given up enough to create a new blade: his first weapon is a charred ruin, the second blazes with light but no heat. (It is unclear if he made another attempt, or if Melisandre just put

> a glamor on the burned blade.) The myths of Azor Ahai say that he ruined two swords in the making.[1]

Clearly his third attempt, with its great sacrifice, has not been made. When it is, he may surprise everyone.

Stannis has Targaryen blood, as his and Robert's Targaryen grandmother gives Robert his claim to the throne. It's very hard to see him as Daenerys's fellow champion and dragonrider, however. Daenerys envisions him in the House of the Undying. "Glowing like sunset, a red sword was raised in the hand of a blue-eyed king who cast no shadow... mother of dragons... slayer of lies..." (II.706). Stannis has blue eyes, and Melisandre creates shades of him out of shadows. He also wields a flaming sword. However, Daenerys, "slayer of lies" may be on a quest to disprove his destiny.

Some people point to the Onion Knight, who is reborn amidst the smoke and salt of the Battle of Blackwater, and rises from near-death to rejoin Stannis. Certainly, it would be ironic if he is Melisandre's chosen one, not Stannis. However, Davos acts steadily as Stannis's advisor, making little effort for world-changing heroism.

1. Jesse Scoble, "A Sword without a Hilt: The Dangers of Magic in (and to) Westeros," Beyond the Wall: Exploring George R. R. Martin's A Song of Ice and Fire, From A Game of Thrones to A Dance with Dragons. (USA: BenBella Books, Inc., 2012). Kindle Edition, Kindle Locations 2056-2060.

Jon dreams of fighting with a blade that "burned red in his fist," (V:769) and Melisandre, staring into her flames, thinks, "I pray for a glimpse of Azor Ahai, and R'hllor shows me only [Jon] Snow" (V:408), suggesting he may be the one. Burned by fire, he discovers how to kill a wight and is rewarded with the hero sword Longclaw, though the salt is less clear in that scene. The stone dragons (on Dragonstone? With the Horn of Winter?) are more intriguing. His Night's Watch oath holds him to be the sword in the darkness, which could literally come true as Azor Ahai.

Jon has also killed Quoron Halfhand for duty, and is no stranger to sacrificing those he loves. However, a larger sacrifice in the future is probably waiting.

> Jon was armored in black ice, but his blade burned red in his fist. As the dead men reached the top of the Wall he sent them down to die again. He slew a greybeard and a beardless boy, a giant, a gaunt man with filed teeth, a girl with thick red hair. Too late he recognized Ygritte. She was gone as quick as she'd appeared. (V:769)

This is Jon's dream, but in it, Jon kills Ygritte and his sword burns red, like Azor Ahai after killing the woman he loves. In the scene he's a warrior of ice and fire joined, defending the Wall.

If he's a Targaryen, he's also heir to the prophecy of the Prince who was Promised, who would be born of the line of Rhaegar and Daenerys's parents—possibly his own grandparents.

In the fifth book, Jon is severely wounded and ends the story on a cliffhanger moment (leaving fans to squabble for years about his eventual fate). Several people have noticed that Jon is being splashed with tears from the giant standing over him, Jon's wound is "smoking" like a dragon's spilled blood, and above him, a dead knight's starry sigil is covered in blood—salt and smoke, a bloody star—here are the Azor Ahai conditions. Even if he dies, he could be revived through many possibilities, from Ghost to Melisandre, and return stronger than before as the destined hero. Some fans suggest he will be put in the cells under the Wall among the *smoking* and *salting* rooms for stored meat, and he may wake the rumored ice dragon sleeping under the ice there, or emerge himself with new magic.

DAENERYS AS CHOSEN ONE

Daenerys was born on Dragonstone, a saltwater-enclosed isle, and then reborn as the Mother of Dragons on a tear-stained smoky funeral pyre. This second birth "woke dragons from stone," and on that morning, the "bleeding star," the Red Comet, appeared. She fits the prophecy better than Stannis or even Jon does. Some readers believe the fiery dragons, born from sacrifice, represent Lightbringer, but the prophecies speak specifically about both dragons and sword, suggesting she'll need one of the magical swords described earlier.

The hero's and heroine's classic journey involves a death-rebirth sequence, bringing the champion back stronger than before.

> These journeys into darkness represent death—only by completely surrendering to the unknown can the heroine transcend her existence, and learn the wisdom and magic of mortality. In ancient matriarchal mythology, this descent was a desirable initiation made by female seekers of knowledge... The power of the ancient feminine would guide a woman down to the world of the unconscious, with untold wisdom as a reward.[2]

Though Dany's mentor is a treacherous and wicked sorceress, she leads her charge through the initiation all heroes must make. This scene in which Daenerys births the dragons is such a moment, emphasizing in epic fantasy style that she is the Chosen One of prophecy and magic. Of course, she will likely have a more devastating death-rebirth sequence further along—in most fantasy epics, the first book and the series as a whole both represent perfect hero's or heroine's journeys.

2. Valerie Estelle Frankel, From Girl to Goddess: The Heroine's Journey through Myth and Legend (Jefferson, NC: McFarland and Co., 2010), 124.

Further, Maester Aemon tells Sam that Daenerys is the child of the prophecy in *A Feast for Crows:* A child of the forest said that "the prince that was promised would be born of their line," the line of Aerys and Rhaella, Daenerys's parents (V:300-301). Maester Aemon notes:

> No one ever looked for a girl. It was a prince that was promised, not a princess. Rhaegar thought … the smoke was from the fire that devoured Summerhall on the day of his birth, the salt from the tears shed for those who died. He shared my belief when he was young, but later he became persuaded that it was his own son who fulfilled the prophecy, for a comet had been seen above King's Landing on the night Aegon was conceived, and Rhaegar was certain the bleeding star had to be a comet.
>
> What fools we were, who thought ourselves so wise! The error crept in from the translation. Dragons are neither male nor female, Barth saw the truth of that, but now one and now the other, as changeable as flame. The language misled us all for a thousand years. (IV:520)

Apparently "prince" is a gender-neutral term in prophecies of the coming champion. Maester Aemon, as one who has lived through more kings than anyone, is shown as unusually perceptive in the series. His theory that Daenerys is the chosen one seems likely. Rhaegar believed it was himself and then his son, but in fact, it's his sister.

BRAN AS CHOSEN ONE

Bran is unlikely to be a warrior, except as a wolf, raven, or possibly dragon. However, it's not a coincidence that he's studying to be a greenseer in the North. He too will play a vital part in the war to come. He could literally ride a dragon—from the first season he learns how to ride again, possibly in preparation for this. (He has green magic, and Rhaegal is a green dragon, in fact.) He is possibly the only hero without any Targaryen blood or mystery about his birth…however, he has incredible magic of his own. He could charm magical animals no one else could manage.

He has two death-rebirth sequences as Jaime pushes him from the tower, then a year later he hides in the crypts as Winterfell burns. Each time, he emerges with a new mission, a new quest he must undertake, all led by the mysterious three-eyed crow. Theon muses, "The gods could not kill Bran, no more than I could" (V.544). So early, he has a destiny.

After Ramsay Bolton razes Winterfell with smoke and possibly salts the earth, Bran crawls from the dark of the crypts. Is this the Azor Ahai prophecy? Did a dragon there awaken? Or one inside Bran as he uses his new powers? Summer, Bran's wolf, sees an intriguing sight, possibly a real dragon, or possibly only an image of one that foreshadows what's to come:

> The smoke and ash clouded his eyes, and in the sky he saw a great winged snake whose roar was a river of flame. He bared his teeth, but then the snake was gone. (II: 956)

Even if he's only seeing the comet, this moment seems significant as a rebirth of sorts and the start of Bran's heroic journey. In the same chapter, Osha notes, "We made enough noise to wake a dragon" (964). Did they?

TYRION AS CHOSEN ONE

Tyrion might choose to ally himself with Daenerys, though he shows loyalty and affection to Myrcella, Tommen, and sometimes Jaime, if not to Cersei, Joffrey, or his father. After his experiences in the series, he may feel the Lannisters would do better at Casterly Rock than on the Iron Throne destroying the kingdom. Or after his time as Hand, he may seek power for himself as Daenerys's advisor.

Of course, becoming Daenerys's ally does not mean he's the Chosen One. He has yet to display talent with magic or prophecy though he's read much about dragons (another piece of evidence he may become Daenerys's counselor).

Some fans doubt Tyrion's paternity: in the book, he has pale blond hair unlike the golden sheen of the other Lannisters. His eyes, one Lannister green and one black, support this as well (Daenerys's classically Targaryen violet eyes are called "nearly black"). Tywin coldly comments: "Men's laws give you the right to bear my name and display my colors, since I cannot prove that you are not mine" (3.1) and Barristan Selmy reports the following to Daenerys:

> "Prince Aerys . . . as a youth, he was taken with a certain lady of Casterly Rock, a cousin of Tywin Lannister. When she and Tywin wed, your father drank too much wine at the wedding feast and was heard to say that it was a great pity that the lord's right to the first night had been abolished. A drunken jape, no more, but Tywin Lannister was not a man to forget such words, or the . . . the liberties your father took during the bedding." (V:577)

These "liberties" could have been anything, and an affair could have taken place later. If so, he could be a Targaryen, heir to their dragon magic and prophecy. It's been emphasized that Daenerys as a Targaryen is immune to traditional illnesses, and Tyrion, exposed to both greyscale and plague, remains conspicuously healthy (for the moment).

However, the series makes more sense if this is another red herring and Tywin's comments are just spite and cruelty. Tyrion is a true Lannister, a brilliant schemer who would have offered much family loyalty if his loved ones hadn't all despised him. This is the great tragedy of his life.

Rhaegar said that his son Aegon was the prince who was promised (II:512). Nonetheless, Rhaegar's obsession with the prophecy may have caused him to misinterpret it as Melisandre does.

A Dance with Dragons provides us a young man who claims to be Aegon Targaryen, switched with another baby before his death and thus the rightful heir (his claim as eldest son of eldest son supersedes Daenerys's claim as Rhaegar's younger sister, if it's true).

Unfortunately, this claim is based on Varys' word that he is the Targaryen child, smuggled from the castle. Any claim based on Varys' word must be considered terribly suspect. Varys has said that he lives to protect the kingdom—a Targaryen heir might bring stability and end the civil war, and decades ago Varys certainly might have wanted to set this up by finding a Targaryen or Volantin bastard with the right appearance and raising him properly. Varys might even make the claim that having an heir to bring stability matters more than his real parentage. He describes Aegon as a fitting heir because he's been groomed that way, unlike so many other kings:

> Aegon has been shaped for rule since before he could walk. He has been trained in arms, as befits a knight to be, but that was not the end of his education. He reads and writes, he speaks several tongues, he has studied history and law and poetry.

> A septa has instructed him in the mysteries of the Faith since he was old enough to understand them. He has lived with fisherfolk, worked with his hands, swum in rivers and mended nets and learned to wash his own clothes at need. He can fish and cook and bind up a wound, he knows what it is like to be hungry, to be hunted, to be afraid...Aegon knows that kingship is his duty, that a king must put his people first, and live and rule for them. (V:958-959)

Whether he's a lowborn child from silvery-haired Volantis, or a descendent from the rebellious Blackfyre bastards who founded the Golden Company, he still could be a hero, even one with Targaryen blood. His storyline has always been planned as he leads the Golden Company to Westeros: A decade before book five's release, Martin wrote, "The Golden Company is the largest and most famous, founded by one of Aegon the Unworthy's bastards. You won't meet them until A DANCE WITH DRAGONS."[3] Whatever his plot arc, he may be crucial.

However, it's problematic from a story perspective that a young man will swoop in and save everyone, becoming a greater hero than Daenerys, Jon, or those we've followed from the beginning. Several visions of "false dragons" and "mummer's [puppeteer's] dragons" add to readers' suspicions.

3. Correspondence with Fans," The Citadel: So Spake Martin, June 3 2000 http://www.westeros.org/Citadel/SSM/Category/C91/P180.

Of course, Aegon may have survived, but be somewhere else, hidden in plain sight...

THREE CHOSEN ONES

There is foreshadowing that Bran, Jon, and Daenerys (among others) may all be the chosen ones who can save Westeros...why not all three?

Daenerys will ride one of her dragons, but she must find two worthy heroes to ride the others, perhaps one companion of action and one of wisdom like her ancestor Aegon the Conqueror had. Jon and Bran are brothers to each other, chosen of the old gods. Bran has no known Targaryen blood, and Jon's origin is a mystery, but their wolf powers of prophecy and animal bonds may be similar to Targaryen powers, only with ice not fire. Bran's powers, like Jon's, could make him more than a dragonrider, but a dragon itself. Perhaps this is the power Daenerys needs to master, so that they can become the three-headed dragon in truth, reviving what Aegon and his sisters only imperfectly echoed.

CHAPTER 4.

DAENERYS'S PROPHECIES

There are more nebulous prophecies made to and about Daenerys than to any other character. Her own dreams and visions, especially in the House of the Undying, show her an immense tapestry of past, present, and future. Quaithe, a Maegi, likewise appears several times to Daenerys and gives her cryptic, riddling advice.

THE STALLION THAT MOUNTS THE WORLD

> "As swift as the wind he rides, and behind him his khalasar covers the earth, men without number, with arakhs shining in their hands like blades of razor grass. Fierce as a storm this prince will be. His enemies will tremble before him, and their wives will weep tears of blood and rend their flesh in grief. The bells in his hair will sing his coming, and the milk men in the stone tents will fear his name." The old woman trembled and looked at Daenerys almost as if she were afraid. "The prince

> is riding, and he shall be the stallion who mounts the world." (I: 411)

Daenerys's son Rhaego was stillborn, so it's assumed the prophecy died with him. Many fantasy series remind readers that human beings have the power to affect prophecy— Daenerys's own choice of trusting the Maegi Mirri Maz Duur and offering her (however unwillingly) her own child as sacrifice likely replaced this prophecy with the ones about the dragons she will ride and her future in Westeros.

Of course, the prophecy of the "prince who was promised" is revealed by Maester Aemon to be gender neutral—Daenerys is the prince. She could potentially be this prince as well, and even lead a khalasar, or another army of "men without number" like the Unsullied. When she is reborn from the fire with her dragons, the prophesized prince arrives. Her "children," the dragons, could also fill this role, though much less literally.

DROGO RETURNS

Upon the stillbirth of her child, Mirri Maz Duur advised her that Drogo will return from his comatose state.

> When the sun rises in the west and sets in the east. When the seas go dry and mountains blow in the wind like leaves. When your womb quickens again,

> and you bear a living child. Then he will return, and not before. (I, Chapter 68)

This may be a curse—a complex way of saying "never." Or as some fans note, it may have come true in the fifth book.

The sun likely refers to the Martell sigil of a sun and spear and Quentin Martell's story in *A Dance with Dragons*. During Daenerys's final chapter in the book, she notes that the Dothraki Sea is drying up in the onrushing autumn. The mountain-shaped pyramids of her city burn down and blow away in the wind. And she bleeds for the first time since she met Khal Drogo…It's either menstruation or a miscarriage, either way suggesting she can become pregnant now. Drogo has already returned in the form of her dragon, his namesake. Or something more literal or in a dream state may occur, now that Daenerys is prepared to bear a living child. When asked if Daenerys is fertile again, Martin comments only, "I am sure Daenerys would like to know. Prophecy can be a tricky business."[1]

THE ARMY OF ICE

> That night she dreamt that she was Rhaegar, riding to the Trident. But she was mounted on a dragon, not a horse. When she saw the Usurper's rebel host

1. Correspondence with Fans," The Citadel: So Spake Martin, Mar 26 2002, http://www.westeros.org/Citadel/SSM/Category/C91/P60).

> across the river they were armored all in ice, but she bathed them in dragonfire and they melted away like dew and turned the Trident into a torrent. Some small part of her knew that she was dreaming, but another part exulted. *This is how it was meant to be. The other was a nightmare, and I have only now awakened.* (III:310)

The host armored in ice could be a suggestion that the battle she should be preparing for is not against the armies of the Seven Kingdoms, but rather of the Others—Dragonfire will prove an important weapon and Dany the destined hero.

DAENERYS FREES THE SLAVES, HOUSE OF THE UNDYING

> Ten thousand slaves lifted bloodstained hands as she raced by on her silver, riding like the wind. "Mother!" they cried. "Mother, mother!" They were reaching for her, touching her, tugging at her cloak, the hem of her skirt, her food, her leg, her breast. They wanted her, needed her, the fire, the life, and Daenerys gasped and opened her arms to give herself to them. (II:707)

This has been fulfilled with Daenerys's liberation of the slaves of Astapor and its neighboring cities in *A Storm of Swords*.

THREE FIRES MUST YOU LIGHT...

> three heads has the dragon . . .

> . . . three fires must you light . . . one for life and one for death and one to love . . .
> . . . three mounts must you ride . . . one to bed and one to dread and one to love . . .
> . . . three treasons will you know . . . once for blood and once for gold and once for love . . .
> (II.515)

This prophecy too comes from the House of the Undying, and Daenerys thinks of it often. Of course, Daenerys's experiences in the first book, from her horse Silver she rides on her wedding night to the Maegi's treason that kills her husband and unborn child to the fire that births her dragons, can be seen fulfilling the first three.

The "dread" is her dragon and the fire for death most likely a cataclysm in war as Drogon burns the enemy into a grisly melted ruin like that of Harrenhal. Hatched from a red and black egg, he even mirrors the Targaryen colors. The fire may already have come true, as there's a great conflagration when she first rides him. However, the third mount is a mystery—what could she ride after a dragon? Perhaps after the war ends, she will find a simpler mount and be, not Khaleesi or Mother of Millions, but simply Daenerys once more. More intriguingly, she might discover her warg magic and ride inside a raven, wolf, or another person—the bonded animal of someone she loves, or an attempt to save someone she loves or return to him.

Treasons are a little clearer: "The Undying of

Qarth had told her she would be thrice betrayed. Mirri Maz Duur had been the first, Ser Jorah the second," Daenerys thinks (V:38). All through the first season, Jorah has been the one informing on her to Varys, and Dany isn't pleased to discover this. This leaves the treason for love.

Azor Ahai "called for his wife, Nissa Nissa, and asked her to bare her breast. He drove his sword into her breast, her soul combining with the steel of the sword, creating Lightbringer" (II:115). This moment must repeat for the great hero to live once again. Further, if Jon or Dany is the great hero, this could fulfill all three terms of the prophecy: If Azor reborn (many signs point to Jon) betrayed his one true love Daenerys and stabbed her to reforge Lightbringer (treason for love), the blade would blaze up in a mighty flame (fire for love), and Daenerys might even be trapped inside the sword as Nissa was, making it her mount for love. Her fire would make the sword a true Lightbringer, combining the love prophecies as the first three were combined. Of course, this would herald a grisly end to Daenerys if she couldn't return through some kind of magic or escape into an animal, her other possible mount for love. "Knowing" three treasons suggests they all will be betrayals of her, but she could be the betrayer and light a pyre under her own true love (whether Jon or someone else), kindling her fire to love as a wrenching sacrifice. Only life can pay for life, so it's certain the chosen one of Westeros will have a hard road.

TO GO NORTH...

Quaithe, Daenerys's sometime magical advisor, appears at Xaro's party on the show and gives Ser Jorah a warning: "I'm no one, but she is the Mother of Dragons. She needs true protectors, now more than ever...They are dragons, fire made flesh. And fire is power" (2.5). In the book, her prophecies are far more riddling and cryptic. She tells Daenerys:

> "To go north, you must go south. To reach the west, you must go east. To go forward you must go back, and to touch the light you must pass beneath the shadow."
>
> Asshai, Daenerys thought. She would have me go to Asshai. "Will the Asshai'i give me an army?" she demanded. "Will there be gold for me in Asshai? Will there be ships? What is there in Asshai that I will not find in Qarth?"
>
> "Truth," said the woman in the mask. And bowing, she faded back into the crowd. (II.426)

Apparently, Daenerys will need something in Asshai, the mysterious land of the Maegi, before she conquers Westeros and the Others (and "touches the light" which may be the sword of Azor Ahai). It may be the Valyrian steel sword she needs to face the Others (of course, Brightroar, the

Lannister sword of fire was lost in Old Valyria, and other famed swords may lie nearby).

A few fans believe Daenerys literally must go East to go West and sail around the world. "Truth" might mean the forgotten lore of Westeros: How to fight the Others, what the Others truly are, what Daenerys's shapechanging power is, why the Targaryens need to be in Westeros, what happened to the dragons long ago.

Certainly, her acts in the Free Cities are a delay of her destiny. It's not surprising Daenerys needs to revert to being the Targaryen heir determined to sail for Westeros and sit on the Iron Throne. In book five she travels alone to the grasslands—beginning her quest to return to the beginning as young Daenerys.

In her Undying House vision, crones from the Dothraki city "knelt shivering before her, their grey heads bowed" (I: 411). Perhaps this will not be fulfilled, as Daenerys's child will not be the Stallion Who Mounts the World—that child died. Or perhaps Daenerys will return to the Dothraki and rule them at last.

DRAGONS OLD AND YOUNG

> "Dragons," Moqorro said in the Common Tongue of Westeros… "Dragons old and young, true and false, bright and dark. And you. A small man with a big shadow, snarling in the midst of all." (V:436)

This last refers to Tyrion, the listener. Whether or not the "shadow" is significant, he will certainly be instrumental in big events. Moqorro is another Maegi, who mingles among characters who leave Westeros and offers a glimmer of their destiny.

Books four and five shows us:

- *Dragons old:* Maester Aemon Targaryen and Bloodraven (both born Targaryens and now over a century old). More details and flashbacks about Aerys are presented as well.
- *and young:* Prince Quentyn Martell who has Targaryen blood, Aegon Targaryen, the alleged lost prince, and Daenerys of course. Possibly Jon Snow.
- *true and false*: Time will tell who is a true Targaryen and who doesn't have what it takes. In this book, Barristan the Bold introduces rumors about Tyrion's mother and Ashara Dayne possibly having bastards, just to muddle things further for readers. More possible heirs to the legacy of Azor Ahai are also introduced.
- *bright and dark:* Jon and Bloodraven are darker than the others. Maester Aemon is blind. Dark may also mean dark of purpose or hidden.

CHAPTER 5.

VISIONS OF THE FUTURE

BRAN'S VISION AFTER HIS CRIPPLING FALL

> He saw his mother sitting alone in a cabin, looking at a bloodstained knife on a table in front of her, as the rowers pulled at their oars and Ser Rodrik leaned across a rail, shaking and heaving. A storm was gathering ahead of them, a vast dark roaring lashed by lightning, but somehow they could not see it.

This section of Bran's dream-vision clearly refers to the danger gathering in King's Landing.

> He saw his father pleading with the king, his face etched with grief. He saw Sansa crying herself to sleep at night, and he saw Arya watching in silence and holding her secrets hard in her heart. There were shadows all around them. One shadow was as dark as ash, with the terrible face of a hound. Another was armored like the sun, golden and beautiful. Over them both loomed a giant in armor made of stone, but when he opened his visor, there

> was nothing inside but darkness and thick black blood.

Based on the events of the series, the three shadows seem clear. The ash-dark shadow with the face of a hound is obviously the Hound, Sandor Clegane. In the golden armor is Jaime Lannister. Littlefinger's family sigil is a stone titan, and he's certainly a danger to Ned and Sansa. However, the giant in armor made of stone is more likely Gregor Clegane, the Mountain that Rides, based on his eventual fate with "darkness and thick black blood." Sandor torments Sansa and Arya, while Jaime's fight with Ned finally leads to his demise. Gregor Clegane fights for the Lannisters and devastates the Stark troops and the Tully countryside. In the second book, he takes Arya prisoner for a time as well.

> He lifted his eyes and saw clear across the narrow sea, to the Free Cities and the green Dothraki sea and beyond, to Vaes Dothrak under its mountain, to the fabled lands of the Jade Sea, to Asshai by the Shadow, where dragons stirred beneath the sunrise.

Asshai still has dragons, if Bran is seeing literally. Daenerys may end up with an army of them instead of only three. Also, Daenerys has already traveled from the free cities to the Dothraki sea to Vaes Dothrak. Since she must go east to reach the west, according to prophecy, she may next journey through the Jade Sea to Asshai.

> Finally he looked north. He saw the Wall shining like blue crystal, and his bastard brother Jon sleeping alone in a cold bed, his skin growing pale and hard as the memory of all warmth fled from him.

Jon's coldness can be read as a metaphor as he suffers and adjusts on the Wall. Or grimmer things may come and he may turn into a wight of sorts.

> North and north and north he looked, to the curtain of light at the end of the world, and then beyond that curtain. He looked deep into the heart of winter, and then he cried out, afraid, and the heat of his tears burned his cheeks.

If the curtain of light at the end of the world is literal, it seems a stronger type of wall meant to keep the Others out. With the return of magic, that curtain may be coming down.

> Now you know, the crow whispered as it sat on his shoulder, now you know why you must live.
>
> "Why?" Bran said, not understanding, falling, falling.
>
> Because winter is coming. (I: 136-137)

Bran hasn't done much to warn his friends about this knowledge, even in the first book, surrounded by allies. If he is not meant to spread the word, he may have a larger role to play as a warrior.

The three-eyed crow seems clear that Bran is the chosen one to fight the Others beyond the curtain—the crow appears to no one else.

JON AND DREAMS

Bran says:

> "I dreamed about the crow again last night. The one with three eyes. He flew into my bedchamber and told me to come with him, so I did. We went down to the crypts. Father was there, and we talked. He was sad."
>
> "And why was that?" Luwin peered through his tube.
>
> "It was something to do about Jon, I think." The dream had been deeply disturbing, more so than any of the other crow dreams. (I:611)

Either the secret of Jon's mother or Jon's grim future is being discussed here. Of course, Jon's fate and birthright are yet to be revealed.

> I'm walking down this long empty hall...opening doors, shouting names...the castle is always empty...the stables are full of bones. That always scares me. I start to run, then, throwing open doors, climbing the tower three steps at a time, screaming for someone, for anyone. And then I find myself in front of the door to the crypts. It's black inside, and I can see the steps spiraling down. Somehow I know I have to go down there, but I don't want to. I'm afraid of what might be waiting for me...I scream that I'm not a Stark, that this isn't my place, but it's no good, I have to go down anyway, so I

> start down, feeling the walls as I descend, with no torch to light the way. It gets darker and darker, until I want to scream...that's when I always wake. (I:224-225)

Jon has a recurring dream of Winterfell, in which the castle is empty (foreshadowing its destruction in the second season). Even the ravens are gone, and the stables are full of bones. Possibly this reflects his actual descent into darkness, terror, and pain, or Lyanna's body down in the crypt is awaiting him with the answers he's sought—he's truly "not a Stark."

CERSEI'S FATE

As a child, Cersei received a prophecy from Maggy the Frog (a mispronunciation of Maegi). Maggy also predicted Cersei's friend, who was there at the time, would not marry Jaime as she wished but would die the next day, as she did—In fact, Melara Hetherspoon "fell" down a well and drowned soon after (IV:413). Since Cersei recalls how her friend "screamed and shouted" in the well (IV:583-584), Cersei clearly pushed her for her effrontery in wanting Jaime and to keep the prophecy secret.

Much of the prophecy about Cersei revealed in *A Feast for Crows* has come true before the series begins:

> Cersei: "When will I wed the prince?"

Maggy: "Never. You will wed the king."

Young Cersei was asking about her planned wedding to Prince Rhaegar—in fact, she weds Robert after he takes the throne.

Cersei: "I will be queen, though?"
Maggy: "Aye. Queen you shall be… until there comes another, younger and more beautiful, to cast you down and take all that you hold dear."

As the story is unfolding, this younger fairer queen might be Sansa, Margaery Tyrell, or Daenerys. Cersei's awareness of this prophecy fuels much of her jealousy towards Joffrey's perspective brides. She spends her time controlling Sansa, whom she views as a protégé of a sort, but Margaery is more willful, with more family support. By the fourth book, her jealousy and paranoia motivate her every action. Some argue Cersei has already been supplanted by this time, but in fact she has not yet reached the ultimate depth of suffering. As with Martin's other characters, good and bad, more pain is to come.

"All she holds dear" is more intriguing. This refers to her children as well as her power, and while she could lose the regency at any time, she will remain Queen Mother until the death of her three children, her only claims to the throne. Without them, the Lannister campaign is doomed. As Tyrion points out, Cersei's one redeeming feature is loving her children (that and her cheekbones) (2.1). Will Sansa, Margaery, or Daenerys kill Cersei's children or cause their deaths through political maneuverings? It is possible. It should also be mentioned that harm comes to Myrcella through the fair young princess Arianne of Dorne and her political maneuvering—perhaps a taste of things to come.

> Cersei: "Will the king and I have children?"
> Maggy: "Oh, aye. Six-and-ten for him, and three for you."

This puzzled Cersei at the time, but between her illegitimate children and Robert's bastards, the situation is clearer.

> Maggy: "Gold shall be their crowns and gold their shrouds."

This suggests all three children will predecease Cersei. (This is hardly surprising given how much animosity Cersei and the Lannisters have earned.) If Joffrey, then Tommen, then Myrcella die, all three would be crowned in the current order of Westeros succession if the Lannisters can maintain the throne that long.

After Joffrey's death, a Myrcella-Tommen civil war with the children both crowned as pawns of Lannister and Dorne is another possibility. In Dorne, the rulers are chosen by birth order, not gender, and Tyrion has sent Myrcella into their control. They have not yet entered the war, but with their massive army, they await the right opportunity.

The first book's image of the two dead Targaryen children, a small boy and girl slaughtered ruthlessly by Tywin Lannister merely for the accident of their royal birth, has reached through the series, and this twisted justice may return to the youngest Lannister children, innocent pawns in the game of thrones.

> Maggy: "And when your tears have drowned you, the valonqar shall wrap his hands about your pale white throat and choke the life from you." (IV:540-541)

The word valonqar means "younger brother." Presumably the phrase means *her* younger brother (rather than famous younger brothers Stannis, Theon, or the Hound, for instance). Jaime and Tyrion are both contenders, as Cersei was born before her twin. While Tyrion and Cersei begin the story with animosity, and Cersei's paranoia focuses on her unloving brother as the threat, she ignores Jaime's wishes in many matters. Jaime slowly becomes disillusioned with his precious sister as the series unfolds and he may well be the culprit, dying alongside her as they were born together. Their lives are tied together far more than most characters. Fans have also speculated about the chain of hands (the books' equivalent of the Hand pin) that one brother or the other might be wearing. The phrasing doesn't indicate an actual person who's Hand of the King, but wording can be terribly ambiguous…

MELISANDRE'S VISIONS

> You are wrong. I have dreamed of your Wall, Jon Snow. Great was the lore that raised it, and great the spells locked beneath its ice. We walk beneath one of the hinges of the world." Melisandre gazed up at it, her breath a warm moist cloud in the air. "This is my place as it is yours, and soon enough you may have grave need of me. Do not refuse my friendship, Jon. I have seen you in the storm, hard-pressed, with enemies on every side. You have so many enemies. Shall I tell you their names?" (V:59)

Clearly, Melisandre understands much of the war that's coming. In fact, she's correct about Jon being surrounded by enemies.

One intriguing scene shows us Melisandre's visions of what is to come on the Wall.

> Skulls. A thousand skulls, and the bastard boy again. Jon Snow…
>
> Yet now she could not even seem to find her king. I pray for a glimpse of Azor Ahai, and R'hllor shows me only Snow. (V:407-408)

Here Melisandre seems to be ignoring the evidence—most readers believe that Jon Snow is Melisandre's destined hero, not Stannis, based on this quote.

> The flames crackled softly, and in their crackling

> she heard the whispered name Jon Snow. His long face floated before her, limned in tongues of red and orange, appearing and disappearing again, a shadow half- seen behind a fluttering curtain. Now he was a man, now a wolf, now a man again. But the skulls were here as well, the skulls were all around him.

Death is all around Jon—certainly many allies, enemies, and loved ones have died near him, back home in Winterfell and on the Wall. The skulls also might be the wights, coming for him. Certainly, he is gaining the ability to transform between man and wolf, but the precise order here may suggest a more important transformation—he will turn into Ghost for some time, and then regain his human form. Seeing him highlighted in flame colors may suggest the Azor Ahai prophecy or that he will turn from a warrior of the ice world into one of ice and fire. The shadow behind the fluttering curtain is also intriguing, as Bran sees a curtain in the first book:

> North and north and north he looked, to the curtain of light at the end of the world, and then beyond that curtain. He looked deep into the heart of winter, and then he cried out, afraid, and the heat of his tears burned his cheeks. (I:137)

Will Jon vanish through the curtain of death? Or travel North, perhaps as a wolf, crow, or spirit to look into the heart of winter as Bran has? A curtain of light to the north is also an odd reversal of the Shadow Daenerys must pass beneath far away, in the land of magic, fire priests, and dragons.

> Snowflakes swirled from a dark sky and ashes rose to meet them, the grey and the white whirling around each other as flaming arrows arced above a wooden wall and dead things shambled silent through the cold, beneath a great grey cliff where fires burned inside a hundred caves. Then the wind rose and the white mist came sweeping in, impossibly cold, and one by one the fires went out. Afterward only the skulls remained. (V:407-408)

In this glimpse, Melisandre is seeing Wildings and the Night Watch in the present, battling wights at Hardholme.

> Visions danced before her, gold and scarlet, flickering, forming and melting and dissolving into one another, shapes strange and terrifying and seductive. She saw the eyeless faces again, staring out at her from sockets weeping blood. Then the towers by the sea, crumbling as the dark tide came sweeping over them, rising from the depths. Shadows in the shape of skulls, skulls that turned to mist, bodies locked together in lust, writhing and rolling and clawing. Through curtains of fire great winged shadows wheeled against a hard blue sky. (V:407-408)

This vision is more cryptic. Rangers blinded and killed certainly suggests the "eyeless faces."

Melisandre definitively says the skulls mean

death, but again, she may be wrong. Many important skulls have been seen in the series:

- The Targaryens' collection of dragon skulls
- The skull delivered to Dorne that may or may not be genuine.
- Rattleshirt, the wilding dressed in bones, and the replacement who wears his armor
- The Golden Company, who dip their dead commanders' skulls in gold and swore to bring them to Westeros.
- The Bridge of Skulls, location of one attack on the Wall, with perhaps another to come.
- Richard Lonmouth, Prince Rhaegar's squire, with a sigil of skulls and kisses (His family hasn't been mentioned since the Harrenhal tournament, so this is unlikely.)
- Seven Skulls, the Ironborn longship, though it's far to the east
- Patchface, Stannis's jester from Volantis—Melisandre says, "Many a time I have glimpsed him in my flames. Sometimes there are skulls about him, and his lips are red with blood." Who is he? Just a mad boy who may commit murder someday? Or a young prophet descended from Targaryens or Maegi?

Any of these could be plot points, but a warning

is likely concerning the dragon skulls (or new dragons from stone) or an invading army—Golden Company, krakens, or wildlings.

The towers by the sea likewise have many possibilities: Melisandre thinks they're Eastwatch, but she notes that they didn't actually look like the same towers (V:416). There are too many towers by the sea to count: The Ironmen raid many towers, including in the Shield Islands (who have a signaling system of watchtowers and wildfire). Old Valyria, Oldtown, and King's Landing have also been suggested. (Melisandre has been to Dragonstone, so it is less likely). A cataclysm like the one that took Old Valyria is also possible.

If the gold and scarlet goes with the bodies writhing in lust, Cersei and Jaime suggest themselves—they and the remaining wildfire in King's Landing may have a part to play in the battle of fire and ice. Death turning into some sort of mist is less clear, though mist occurs when fire and ice or fire and seawater mix. Spirits are also a possibility. The winged shadows appear to be dragons returning to Westeros, though Daenerys must travel to the Shadow before this can come.

PART 3.

THE INFLUENCES OF HISTORY

CHAPTER 6.

THE OLD GODS AND THE NEW: RELIGION RETOLD

THE GODSWOOD

"The singers of the forest had no books. No ink, no parchment, no written language...When they died, they went into the wood, into leaf and limb and root, and the trees remembered" (V:452). Just as little is known about the ancient druids, who left no written records. Their sacred places remain as stone circles, ancient caves, and patterns of oak leaves, much like the heart trees whose true origins have been lost to time.

Theon smirks that Ned Stark "prayed to a tree" (II:75). Likewise, Celts saw the world around them as sacred and were particularly close to their holy trees: "Rocks, mountains, groves, and even individual trees were not only sites of worship but sacred in themselves."[1] Druidic ceremonies took place under the open sky or in sacred groves. Pliny said of the Celts: "They choose oak-woods for their sacred groves, and perform no sacred rite without using oak branches."[2] They also revered yew, rowan, and mistletoe, whose red cones and berries echo the red leaves of the weirwood groves. Clearly the Old Religion is meant to be the druids, threatened by the coming of newer religions.

They believed that spirits could inhabit the bodies of people and animals, and even manifest themselves as the spirits of places like wells and caves. In fact, the mysterious Children of the Wood, Martin's elves of a sort along with the mysterious greenseers, tie their souls to the trees and used them to watch the world. Their echo still lingers in trees and crows as these place spirits, protecting the world. Meera Reed describes her father as man of the old ways, strong with nature magic, explaining, "He could talk to trees and weave words and make castles appear and disappear" (III:337). As such, he sounds like a folkloric trickster out of Celtic myth. He even visits the green men, who might or might not be the children of the wood.

Bran has a vision of times long past, with the Starks offering human sacrifice in the Godswood

1. John King, The Celtic Druids' Year (USA: Sterling Publishing Co., 1994), 20-21.
2. P.W. Joyce, A Social History of Ancient Ireland (London, 1903), i. 236; MacCulloch, The Religion of the Ancient Celts,(Edinburgh: T. and T. Clark, 1911), 201.

like the druids, dangling entrails from the heart trees. It is written:

> The Celts made their sacred places in dark groves, the trees being hung with offerings or with the heads of victims. Human sacrifices were hung or impaled on trees, *e.g.* by the warriors of Boudicca. These, like the offerings still placed by the folk on sacred trees, were attached to them because the trees were the abode of spirits or divinities who in many cases had power over vegetation.[3]

The old religions have their darker side, as they honor their gods with blood as well as peace and stillness.

Shapeshifting was also common in Celtic legend. Werewolves of the region, known as *faoladh* or *conroicht,* were considered kindly protectors and guardians of mankind.

> During the whole time that an Ossorian lived as a wolf, his own proper body remained at home as if he were dead: and when about to make a wolf of himself he gave strict orders to his friends not to disturb the body; for if it were removed he was never able to regain his own shape, but was doomed to remain a wolf for the rest of his natural life. While he was in his wolf-shape he ravaged sheep-folds and devoured cattle, and was in every respect as fierce and bloodthirsty as any natural-born wolf. And if you came on him suddenly and attacked him in the act of eating a sheep, he

3. J. A. MacCulloch, The Religion of the Ancient Celts, 198.

> commonly ran straight home and resumed his own shape.[4]

This is the type of wolf Bran can become: preying on animals but helpful to mankind. His human form remains in bed, "as if he were dead," while his mind travels in the wolf. Druidic tradition also has the dead appearing in dreams with prophecies and warnings. Bran and Rickon, like Jon, dream of their father's death through their wolf magic.

When a fan asked Martin if all the Stark children are skin changers with their wolves, he replied, "To a greater or lesser degree, yes, but the amount of control varies widely," adding also that "Bran and Summer are somewhat of a special case."[5] In fact, Jon too begins to see through his wolf's eyes. He is the one at the series' beginning to notice the direwolves match the number and sex of the Stark children, and he finds the near-invisible white runt hidden in the snow.

Celtic and Welsh myths often begin with mystical white animals appearing to the hero from the Otherworld, from King Arthur's white deer to Pryderi and Manawydan's gleaming white boar and the mysterious White Hound of the Mountain. Jon notices that Ghost with his white fur and red eyes has similar coloring to the wierwood trees, white with red leaves (V:466).

4. P.W. Joyce, "The Man-Wolves of Ossory," The Wonders of Ireland (1911). http://www.libraryireland.com/Wonders/Man-Wolves.php.
5. Correspondence with Fans," The Citadel: So Spake Martin, Feb 12 2001. http://www.westeros.org/Citadel/SSM/Category/C91/P120.

He's clearly one of those Otherworld guides. With Ghost beside him, Jon has prophetic shapechanger dreams—he sees Bran with a third eye, and in his dream, the heart tree gives him one as well, even as he enters Ghost and hears his thoughts (II:559-561). On the Wall, savaged by wights and supernatural creatures, Jon particularly depends on his wolf's senses (in contrast to Robb, who often ignores his wolf's warnings).

THE DROWNED GOD

Viking and Saxon raiders attacked both Celts and Christians through the centuries. The raiders worshipped Odin and the Norse gods, and believed they would feast in Valhalla after they died. The Ironborn, too, speak of feasting forever in the Drowned God's halls. The concepts of "drowning" newborns momentarily in the sea and the "god who died for us" seem Christian on the surface. However, they have strong correspondences with Celtic belief.

The Celts had a feast hall like Valhalla, named *buriden*. The pre-Christian Druids likewise dipped their children in rivers to protect them from fairies and the Otherworld. Celtic heroes such as Ailill in the Irish epic *The Tain* was "baptized in Druidic streams," as the hero Gwri was "baptized with the baptism which was usual at that time."[6]

6. MacCulloch, The Religion of the Ancient Celts, 309-310

"What is dead may never die, but rises again, harder and stronger," the priests chant. The Celts too believed in resurrection, with their spirits retuning through the natural world. The Celts even drowned people in sacrifice to their harsh sea gods Manannan, Morgen, and Dylan. Some Celtic warriors would draw weapons and battle the onrushing waves "with sword and spear, often perishing in the rushing waters rather than retreat."[7]

The Iron Islanders were First Men and their religion, like that of the Old Gods, dates to before the Andal Invasion with its newer religion. The Drowned Men, in their sea-colored robes of mottled green, grey, and blue with driftwood cudgels echo the wise yet cryptic druids, guardians of the old ways. The blessing of "Bless him with salt, bless him with stone, bless him with steel" echoes the oaths Celts would make to the elements like "sea, stone, and sky." Their harmony with nature has particularly Celtic echoes.

CHRISTIANITY ARRIVES

The Great Sept of Baelor was founded by King Baelor the Blessed, an overly pious king like Edward the Confessor of England. Both were known for excessive fasting, chastity even within marriage, charity, humility, and religious devotion

7. Ibid. 178.

at the cost of worldly rule (IV:457). In fact, both were considered saints in their time. Baelor the Blessed, as he was known, had the Great Sept of King's Landing renamed as the Great Sept of Baelor in his honor.

One legend described Baelor walking barefoot into a viper's nest to rescue his cousin Aemon, and the vipers refused to bite him. Baelor thus secured an alliance with Dorne, though some said the venom had driven him mad. Frightened of his own lust, Baelor locked his sister-wife Daena and his younger sisters in the area of the palace that became known as the Maidenvault. He spent the rest of his days in pious prayer, leaving his uncle to run the kingdom as Hand. When he fasted and purged too severely, he perished. (III Chapter 6 Sansa, Chapter 59, Sansa.)

Ned is executed on the steps of the Great Sept of Baelor (a deed later revealed as insulting to the Septons) and Arya watches from her perch on a statue of Baelor. The Sept shares many features with European cathedrals, from church bells to stained glass windows. Inside, altars to the seven gods glimmer in candlelight like saints' shrines. In the catacombs below lie royal tombs. Martin notes, "Some local septons are not very well educated (like priests in medieval Europe), but there are great centers of religious training, and the Great Sept of Baelor would certainly be preeminent among them."[8]

The new seven-part gods who are different aspects of a single one deliberately reflect the Catholic trinity, as Martin has discussed in interviews. Maid, Mother, and Crone are a common goddess split among female life stages, while Father, Warrior, and Smith likewise divide the men by role in the world. Left behind is the ominous dark god, the androgynous Stranger, "less and more than human, unknown and unknowable" (II:372). His/her face is a shadowy black oval with stars for eyes. Though this form is ominous, its mysteriousness echoes the Holy Spirit, along with providing a focus for outcasts: Tyrion considers himself the stranger and lights a candle to it (II:477).

Much like Christianity in our world, the faith is fully integrated into life in Westeros, from trial by combat to casual expletives and sacred oaths. Knights are expected to take oaths of the Seven (thus followers of the Old Gods do not precisely become knights). The High Septon anoints the king, and his support is essential for the monarchy. He himself echoes the pope or archbishop, with crowns, rings, and vestments of his office. Below him are Septons, brothers, and sisters, sparrows, and so forth, much like the ranks of the Catholic Church. The Seven-Pointed Star is the chief holy text, echoing the Bible. In the fourth

8. Correspondence with Fans," The Citadel: So Spake Martin, June 3 2000. http://www.westeros.org/Citadel/SSM/Category/C91/P180/

book, the Faith's emerging power likely alludes to an era of religious warfare and violence ranging from the Crusades to the Inquisition.

Of course, the arrival of the Andals with their seven-part god signaled the fading of the Old Gods through both war and neglect:

> When men arrived, they burned the woods and protective faces. The children fought, and the greenseers made the waters rise, smashing the Broken Arm of Dorne that had enabled men to cross. But the men, armed with bronze, were winning. At last, men and children signed the Pact: men would live in the coastlands and meadows, the children now they live only in dreams would take the deep woods…The Andals brought the new gods and conquered all but the north. (I:736-37)

The druids too lost their groves as the Christians gained influence.

> Tree-worship was rooted in the oldest nature worship, and the Church had the utmost difficulty in suppressing it. Councils fulminated against the cult of trees, against offerings to them or the placing of lights before them and before wells or stones, and against the belief that certain trees were too sacred to be cut down or burned. Heavy fines were levied against those who practised these rites, yet still they continued. … S. Martin of Tours was allowed to destroy a temple, but the people would not permit him to attack a much venerated pine-tree which stood beside it–an excellent example of the way in which the more official paganism fell before Christianity, while the older religion of the

soil, from which it sprang, could not be entirely eradicated.[9]

Tacitus tells us that the druids' sacred groves were destroyed at the time of the conquest. In just this way, the advent of the new gods sees the abandonment of the heart trees, while Melisandre and her red god set fire to sacred groves, tearing them from the earth.

The Old Gods are losing power as the Godswoods vanish one by one. However, they hold the power to save Westeros, if the heroes can see it in time.

R'HLLOR AND THE PERSIANS

For the origins of R'hllor and the red priests, we must look to the Zoroastrians of Persia. There, Ahura Mazda is the lord of light and wisdom, creator of the universe. His opposite is Angra Mainyu, creator of evil in mankind, lord of darkness. Here is the source of R'hllor of light and the "Other" of darkness. Followers of Ahura Mazda directly worshipped fire, proclaiming it the son of the god. Ahura Mazda's cult of the sacred fire was famed for "bringing clear guidance and joy to the true believer but destruction to lovers of evil."[10] Likewise, R'hllor's priests call him

9. MacCulloch, The Religion of the Ancient Celts, 203-204.
10. O. Nigosian, The Zoroastrian Faith: Tradition and Modern Research (Canada: McGill-Queens University Press, 2003), 21.

"the Heart of Fire, the God of Flame and Shadow," a source of prophecy and true vision (II.20).

Zoroastrianism encouraged proselytizing and conversion, insisting like the red priests that other religions should be wiped out. The Zoroastrians also believed in a type of resurrection in which "the bones of the physical body would be raised up, and, clothed in immortal flesh, be united with the soul in heaven."[11] The priests of R'hllor can do resurrection of a type, breathing flame into the dead and reanimating them. The Persians also used their fires to bring healing and purification, as Melisandre does. "The night is dark and full of terrors, old man, but the fire burns them all away," she notes (2.1).

A further, even more blatant connection between these faiths is the word "Maegi," source of the modern words "magic" and "magician" but also of the Magi at the birth of Jesus.[12] The Maegi "performed certain rituals and ceremonies connected with fire, sacrifices and burials" and "may have claimed supernatural knowledge and acted as fortune-tellers, astrologers, magicians, sorcerers, tricksters, and charlatans."[13] Maegi seen in Martin's series include prophets who appear to Daenerys, Arya, and Cersei, royal advisors like Melisandre, and known charlatans like Thoros,

11. Mary Boyce, Zoroastrians: Their Religious Beliefs and Practices (London: Routledge & Kegan, 1979), 14.
12. King, The Celtic Druids' Year, 21.
13. Nigosian, The Zoroastrian Faith, 8.

who lights a sword with wildfire and performs in tournaments. He admits later that he had no powers before the comet arrived and magic returned to the world.

The prophet Zoroaster himself wrote of a future battle when a great crisis shall threaten the world and finally bring about its rebirth. After a miraculous virgin birth, the hero called the Saoshyant would arise to lead the final battle and drive evil from the world. It is written:

> He will be the "son of a virgin" and the "All-conquering." His name shall be the Victorious (verethrajan), Righteousness-incarnate (astvat-ereta), and the Saviour (saoshyant). Then the living shall become immortal, yet their bodies will be transfigured so that they will cast no shadows, and the dead shall rise, "within their lifeless bodies incorporate life shall be restored."[14]

The metal of the mountains will melt into a great flaming river, and the wicked will be destroyed forever. This sounds much like Melisandre's search for Azor Ahai and his flaming sword as the Others threaten the world of Westeros.

As the contrasting religions of our world battle on the stage of Westeros, each claims to follow the one true way, even the people of Braavos with its thousand different gods. Melisandre insists she has come to lead the great battle against the Other,

14. Paul Carus, History of the Devil (USA: Open Court, 1900), 58. The Sacred Texts Archive. http://www.sacred-texts.com/evil/hod/index.htm.

but as a fundamentalist, she does it by burning statues of the Seven and weirwood groves, to say nothing of human sacrifice. Only the end of the saga can reveal whether her inspiration derives from the true powers of Westeros or from her own delusions and misinterpretations. Will the children of the forest offer the key to their world's salvation? Or is the secret held by the Faceless Men or Asshai beneath the Shadow? Time will tell.

CHAPTER 7.

HENRY TUDOR, PRINCE WHO WAS PROMISED, AND ENGLISH HISTORY

Westeros is medieval England, basically speaking. They hold tournaments with a Queen of Love and Beauty and trial by combat. As characters travel, they come across the ruins of Harrenhal, burned by dragonfire in Aegon's conquest, or encounter an ancestor's banner in a basement. Everywhere is the history of ages past, in a romanticized way America lacks. Martin comments:

> In 1981, on my first trip outside the United States, I visited England to see my old friend and writer Lisa Tuttle. I spent a month there and we went through the country visiting the most important sites. And when we were to Scotland we visited Hadrian's Wall. I remember it was the end of the day, near sunset. The tour buses were leaving and we have the wall nearly for ourselves. It was fall and the wind was blowing. When we arrive on the top, I tried to imagine how would be the life of a roman legionary of the first or second century after Christ.

> That wall was the edge of the known world, and it was protecting the cities from the enemies behind the wall. I experienced a lot of feelings there, looking to the North, and I just used it when I started to write Game of Thrones. However, fantasy needs an active imagination. I couldn't just describe Hadrian's Wall. It is pretty amazing but it's about ten feet tall and it's made of stone and mud. Fantasy requires more magnificent structures so I exaggerated the attributes of Hadrian's Wall.

The Wildings are much like the Scots—loosely knit tribes feared by those in "civilized lands" as barbarians. While the conquerors from overseas took over the continent, they stopped at the Wall and built it to keep out those too savage to rule.

The ancient conquerors of Westeros have historical parallels, as they do with the Celts and Christians. Many would call the "First Men" equivalent to the Celts, with the seven kingdoms of the Andals as the Saxons' seven kingdoms in England. They come from the same place as the Germanic Vandals who pillaged the Roman Empire—The Romans in turn, are seen in the ruins and lost technology of Old Volantis from roads to forged metals. In this scenario, the most recent invaders are the Targaryens or Normans, the successful conquerors of the continent. Martin supports this when he notes that Aegon the Conqueror derives from William the Conqueror, the Norman leader who made himself king of England.[1] The British culture we know, from modern English to the classical roots of society, is built on this progression, with the Normans the final conquerors.

The trappings of the series: knights, chivalry, feudalism, noble houses with shield emblems and mottos, all derive from England, as do many Westerosi names such as Sir James Tyrell, the supposed murderer of the English princes in the tower. Jon, Robert, Edmund, Edward/Eddard, Richard/Rickard, Jane/Jeyne, Geoffrey/Joffrey, James/Jaime, Margret/Margaery, Marcella/Myrcella, Thomas/Tommen, Caitlyn/Catelyn, Lisa/Lysa, and Walter/Walder are English names that appear often in the chronicle of medieval England as they do in *Game of Thrones*. (Bran or Brandon by contrast is an Irish name meaning raven or crow.) The Warden of the East, Warden of the West, etc. were important positions in England as well as Westeros.

The Black Plague (appearing first in England in 1348 with several subsequent returns) caused shortages of labor and crops. With feudalism ended, the new system allowed great lords to order minor lords to supply them with troops, equipping them for massive battles, as likewise seen in *Game of Thrones.* Soldiers turned mercenaries after the wars in France likewise supplied extra soldiers eager for battle. While

1. "Correspondence with Fans," The Citadel: So Spake Martin, Aug 15 2001. http://www.westeros.org/Citadel/SSM/Category/C91/P90

plague is seen occasionally in Martin's series, the coming of winter is shown as the threat to crops and lives. A famine is certain, as the people of Westeros have been warring rather than planting.

YORK AND LANCASTER

While other parallels appear, the War of the Five Kings, especially the Houses of Stark and Lannister, appears to be a retelling of the English Wars of the Roses (1455–85), between the Houses of Lancaster and York for the English throne. York's emblem was the white rose, and Lancaster's the red.

Both houses claimed the throne through descent from the sons of Edward III: York and Lancaster were cousins, and the many repeated family names add confusion to the tale. The Yorks dwelt in the north of England, with the Lancasters farther south.

Rulers of England

House of Lancaster

Henry IV ("Bolingbroke," son of the Duke of Lancaster), 1399-1413.

Henry V (son of Henry IV), 1413-1422.

Henry VI (son of Henry V, deposed), 1422-1471.

Henry VII (The last scion of this house, raised overseas) 1485-1509

House of York:

Edward IV (son of the Duke of York), 1461-1483.

Edward V (son of Edward IV), 1483.

Richard III ("Crookback," brother of Edward IV) 1483-1485

Margaret of Anjou, French queen-consort to Henry VI, arguably began the War of the Roses, determined to keep the Duke of York from displacing her family or stealing her regency. Like Cersei, she ruled through a mad young puppet king, battling his corrupt advisors to keep his and her power. In fact, the madness seen in children of incest, like Joffrey and the Targaryens, reflects the madness of many European royal houses of the time—for the same reason.

Margaret's husband, Henry VI, had ascended to the throne as the age of six months, supervised by a regent council. After his heroic father, Henry V, near-miraculous winner of the Battle of Agincourt, the son was a disappointment to the people. Worse, after gaining his majority, he remained hopelessly childlike, agreeing placidly to every proposal put before him. In personality he seemed much like Cersei's youngest son Tommen, tractable and obedient to everyone else's desires. With no initiative and no desire to make war, Henry let his father's hard-won French territories be reclaimed. And after a particularly shocking loss, he slipped into a catatonic state, "taken and smitten with a frenzy and his wit and reason withdrawn."[2]

Margaret took charge of many of his duties. Like Cersei, Margaret found herself ruling through her young son and encouraging his violence. In an incident particularly reminiscent of Lysa Arryn and her son or the bloodthirsty Joffrey, Margaret of Anjou put two knights on trial and asked her son their fate. He ordered beheading.

Sixteen months later, the king recovered and asked the name of his young son, Prince Edward, who'd been brought to greet him. This son, born after eight years of childless marriage, left his mother open to speculation and rumor, much like Cersei's conspicuously blond children. Leading the spread of these rumors was Richard Plantagenet, Duke of York, who, like Stannis, stood next in line.

The Duke of York has interesting parallels with Ned Stark—Richard's father, the Earl of Cambridge, was beheaded for rebelling against the previous king, King Henry V. He was fostered by Ralph de Neville, Warden of the West March as Jon Arryn was Warden of the East. It was de Neville's job, among other things, to guard Hadrian's Wall. The earls in York's neighboring Northumberland were famed as the "Kings in the

2. Bale's Chronicle, qtd. in Helen Castor, She-Wolves: The Women Who Ruled England before Elizabeth (New York: Harper, 2011), 345.

North," a region they ran almost as a hereditary domain.

York marched on London, but his army was outnumbered and he had little support from the nobles. Thus York, like Ned Stark, was placed under house arrest in London and compelled to swear allegiance to the king. However, after the king's catatonia, York had another chance. A powerful baronial clique, backed by Ralph Neville's son Richard, the Earl of Warwick and called the "kingmaker," installed his foster-brother Richard, Duke of York, as "Protector of the Realm" and regent, much as Ned Stark was appointed for the new and unsuited King Joffrey. After the Duke of York went so far as to proclaim himself king, he was named Henry's heir in a compromise.

As Margaret refused to let her child be swept aside, the land divided into north and south. When Henry supported Margaret, York took up arms for self-protection and matters escalated. The first battle at St. Albans in 1455 resulted in a Yorkist victory and four years of uneasy truce. Civil war resumed in 1459. The Lancastrians surprised and killed York at Wakefield in December, much as Ned dies and leaves the war to his son. In fact, York's head was stuck on a pike by the Lancastrian armies, though it was removed and buried later.

York's eldest son and heir, Edward, defeated a Lancastrian force at Mortimer's Cross and raced to London, beating Margaret's forces. He was crowned King Edward IV at Westminster. He then pursued Margaret to Towton and won a terribly bloody battle there. A last attempt to claim the throne saw her son, Edward, now seventeen, dying in battle at Tewkesbury, in a heroic moment echoing Rhaegar's last stand. His father, Henry VI was quietly executed in the Tower of London, and Margaret went into exile. The Lancaster line had become extinguished, save for Henry Tudor (the future Henry VII), living in exile across the sea, like Viserys and Daenerys.

KING ROBERT RETOLD

King Edward IV began a time of peace and prosperity, but he was overfond of pleasure and revelry, much like King Robert Baratheon, who's based on him, as Martin admits. [3] Though an active fighter, after the war, he became indolent, caring more for pleasure than politics. He craved popularity, which he cultivated through exotic entertainments as well as his fine manners.

Of course, Martin notes that his characters may be inspired from history, but he takes care to make them his own:

> You can do one-for-one conversions of the real-world to fantasy, but if you're going to do one-for-

3. "Correspondence with Fans," The Citadel: So Spake Martin, Aug 15 2001. http://www.westeros.org/Citadel/SSM/Category/C91/P90

> one, you might as well just write straight historical fiction. Why write about a character who's exactly like Henry VIII? If you want to do that, then just write about Henry VIII.
>
> It makes more sense to take certain interesting elements of Henry VIII and certain interesting elements of Edward IV, and maybe something from here and something from there, and put them together and use your imagination to create your own character—someone who is uniquely himself and not exactly like someone from history. The same is true of the battles and things like that.[4]

Certainly King Edward's descendent Henry VIII was also quite fat, fond of feasting and wenching rather than conquering.

King Edward was actually absent from his final victory as he was busy contracting a secret marriage with Elizabeth, daughter of Richard Woodville, Lord Rivers. Politically, this was a weak choice, compared with the French princess King Edward's advisors were suggesting. (Robb makes a similarly unpolitical marriage in the second season, though King Edward's was one of many in history.) Edward went on to honor and promote his new in-laws, causing even more vexation. One earl even led a rebellion over the unpopularity of the Woodvilles.

4. Josh Roberts, "Game of Thrones' Exclusive! George R.R. Martin Talks Season Two, 'The Winds of Winter,' and Real-World Influences for 'A Song of Ice and Fire,'" Smarter Travel, April 1, 2012. http://www.smartertravel.com/blogs/today-in-travel/game-of-thrones-exclusive-george-martin-talks-season-the-winds-of-winter-and-real-world-influences-for-song-of-ice-and-fire.html?id=10593041.

In his last years he was given to self-indulgence and scandalous excesses. He remained popular, even as he sported with his courtiers' wives and produced numerous bastards. When he died suddenly at age 41, thanks to his stout and inactive lifestyle, illness, or possibly poison, the realm was suddenly destabilized. Like Robert Baratheon, Edward had two brothers who both craved power—one hastily seized power after arranging for his more charming brother's execution. This cruel brother, known to history and literature as Shakespeare's villainous Richard III, had the two princes, Edward V and Richard of York, declared illegitimate. As Lord Protector and regent, he locked them in the Tower of London, where they died under mysterious circumstances. Some readers equate Bran and Rickon, apparently murdered to destroy their claim to Winterfell, with these princes.

At last, the future Henry VII sailed from over the sea and battled Richard III's forces at Bosworth Field in 1485. Victorious, he wed Edward IV's eldest daughter, Elizabeth, and united the red and white roses to create the Tudor Rose, ending the long feud.

Cersei as Margaret and Robert as Edward IV are close analogies. Likewise, the realm in chaos at King Robert's death, with his children declared bastards and Starks and Lannisters vying for the throne echoes this time period.

How will this all end? It's unclear. Richard, Duke of York (basically the Ned Stark character) never inherited England, but his sons Edward IV and Richard III did, followed by Edward's daughter Elizabeth. Will Ned's son Jon Snow inherit such a destiny, ending the war by wedding the Targaryen heir, Daenerys? Martin notes, "The Lancasters and Yorks fought themselves to extinction until the Tudors came in. But the Tudors were really a new dynasty; they weren't Lancasters. So…"[5]

The War of the Roses ended with a dynastic wedding, with the last scions uniting Lancaster and York and taking the throne. Could this be Sansa and Tyrion? Neither is in the succession for the Iron Throne, but they could decide to stay together, have children, and heal their shattered houses. Tyrion has always wanted someone to love and accept the real him, while Sansa has been blinded by dazzling unworthy knights like Joffrey and Ser Loras. Perhaps they will learn enough to find peace together.

5. "A Very Long Interview with George R.R. Martin."

CHAPTER 8.

WOMEN'S ROLES IN HISTORY AND WESTEROS

Throughout history, women have been part of the "oldest profession" as it's known (though not with full Brazilian waxes). Just about every episode shows bare breasts, and nudity is explicitly tied with subjugation: women strip to manipulate men, as if sex is all they have to offer. Non-prostitute characters, like Melisandre the priestess and Osha the wildling, likewise strip and have sex with the men to control them. Even Daenerys, the amazing conqueror and chosen one, starts as a raped, fully nude child-bride who asks her maid for sex lessons to better deal with her husband.

The very few characters who keep their clothes on at all times (Catelyn, Brienne, Yara, Arya, and Sansa) try to find a different way to manage in a patriarchal world. And in many cases, they do. Martin notes:

> I wanted to present my female characters in great diversity, even in a society as sexist and patriarchal as the Seven Kingdoms of Westeros. Women would find different roles and different personalities, so women with different talents would find ways to work with it in a society according to who they are.[1]

Indeed, all the show's women, from Queen Cersei to Yara Greyjoy, make different points about what it's like to be a woman in their society. In medieval England, women were bartered as marriage pawns and expected to care for their husbands and families as their only profession. A few, especially widows like Lysa, Cersei, and Catelyn, found a road to a different kind of power, claiming regencies and inciting wars. While the medieval world saw isolated female pirates, mercenary captains, and brave peasant girls seeking individual glory, the highborn ladies who led armies in war could and did change the face of history as they played the Game of Thrones. In context, how accurate are the women of Westeros?

LADY SANSA

Of course, political marriages were typical for young women—very young women in some cases. They often married at the onset of puberty, at

1. Ibid.

12-13, and normally before 20; the average age was between 15 and 16. In the first book, Sansa is 11 (13 on the show) and she's already betrothed to Joffrey. As Daenerys, thirteen and quickly pregnant in the first book, discovers, there are no adolescents or teenagers in medieval times—only children and women. When a woman was able to have children herself, a match was made for her. As Cersei, Sansa, and the Tyrell ladies intrigue in King's Landing, they parallel many European queens wed for their lands but eager to do more than bear children.

With her constant insistence on "courtesy as a lady's armor," Sansa demonstrates her love for medieval "courtesy books"—primers on proper behavior written mainly between the twelfth and fifteenth centuries. While many were written by men, one famous set was penned by the early feminist Christine de Pizan. She writes:

> It seems to me that it is the duty of every princess and high-born lady, excelling in honour and status above all others, to excel in goodness, wisdom, manners, temperament and conduct, so that she can serve as an example on which other ladies and all other women can model their behaviour. Thus it is fitting that she should be devoted to God and have a calm, gentle and tranquil manner, restrained in her amusements and never intemperate.[2]

2. Christine de Pizan, Le Livre des Trois Vertus, trans. Garay and Jeay (Paris: H. Champion, 1989), 139-147. http://mw.mcmaster.ca/scriptorium/cdpizan2.html.

By acting such, the queen could provide a comforting role model, as Sansa does while leading the women in prayer during Stannis's siege. Further, she could provide a civilizing influence on her husband. This is how first-season Sansa sees herself, as Joffrey's lady and gentling influence. De Pizan advises ladies with husbands who "conduct themselves abominably" to "bear all this and to dissemble" for responding harshly will gain her nothing.[3] It's clear as the series unfolds that Sansa means to take this advice.

Traditional queen consorts took the role of intercessor, publicly pleading with the king to show mercy on behalf of a particular petitioner "to soften his heart toward his subjects and improve his rule."[4] Of course, in "The Pointy End," Sansa kneels before the court, beautifully dressed and graceful. She words a pretty plea, allowing Joffrey to excuse her father for love of her. In fact, traditional intercession was generally arranged in advance, allowing the king to seem merciful but not weak, yielding only to his lady's pleas. As the queen's role declined through the 9th to 12th centuries, the intercession remained her greatest, possibly only path to public and private power.

3. Cyte of Ladyes sig. ff iv, qtd. in Diane Bornstein, The Lady in the Tower: Medieval Courtesy Literature for Women (Hamden, Connecticut; Archon Books, 1983), 69.
4. John Carmi Parsons "The Queen's Intercession in Thirteenth-Century England," Power of the Weak: Studies on Medieval Women, eds. Jennifer Carpenter and Sally-Beth MacLean (Chicago: University of Illinois Press, 1995), 147.

Joffrey, of course, ignores what's expected of a merciful and politically astute king to execute Ned Stark in front of a shocked Sansa's eyes. Even the small influence accorded her by medieval tradition and courtesy books has been denied to her, publicly hurled in her face. It's no wonder she faints in horror.

In the following season, she learns courtly craftiness, manipulating Joffrey into sparing a drunken knight. (In the books, she and Ser Dontos subsequently engage in a courtly love drama, in which he swears to be "her knight" and protect her.) As Joffrey rides off to the Battle of Blackwater, Sansa slyly adds that her brother would be in the vanguard of the fighting and she knows Joffrey will do the same. Her place at court is finally usurped by Margaery Tyrell, who proves Sansa's superior at manipulating Joffrey. This subtle kind of power was expected of court ladies, just as the intercession was.

"Margaery has her claws in Joffrey. She knows how to manipulate him," Cersei complains jealously.

"Good, I wish you knew how to manipulate him," Lord Tywin responds, clearly eager to have his grandson rule in name only while a strong woman guides him from behind the throne (2.4). Though the king might rule, his people knew whose voice made the final decisions.

Lady knights like Brienne are one of the more atypical archetypes, though a few existed in European history: Louise Labé, a ropemaker's daughter born in 1520 Lyon, France, jousted in tournaments, naming herself "La Belle Amazon" and "Capitaine Louise." In her poetry, she cried for women to "raise their minds slightly, above their falstaffs and bobbins."[5] Some (possibly exaggerated) tales of the time even see her fighting the Spanish in battle. Joan of Arc of course is famous for dressing in a knight's garb and crowning the King of France. In battle she led the charges, sword raised. As a result, however, she was accused of being a witch, a prostitute, and a cross-dresser, and finally burned at the stake.

Men of their time weren't encouraging of women fighting beside them. Martin notes, "The women in fantasy tend to be very atypical women…They tend to be the woman warrior or the spunky princess who wouldn't accept what her father lays down, and I have those archetypes in my books as well [as more historical ones]."[6] "I'm-no-Lady" Brienne is such an atypical figure.

When historical women did go to battle, especially peasant women, they generally

5. "Louise Labé" Encyclopedia of Women in the Renaissance: Italy, France, and England, eds. Diana Maury Robin, Anne R. Larsen, and Carole Levin (USA: ABC-CLEO, 2007), 195-198.
6. "A Very Long Interview with George R.R. Martin."

disguised themselves as men. Tales of these disguised women are spread throughout the world, from the Ballad of Mulan to tales of Sarah Bishop and other Revolutionary War soldiers. They were celebrated for their bravery, but their gender was usually only revealed after their triumph. On the show of course, Brienne wins her tournament against Ser Loras, is named the victor, and only then removes her helmet. Perhaps she's noticed that if she declares herself a woman, she's less likely to be acclaimed for her skills.

Actual knighthood (offered to neither Louise Labé nor Joan of Arc) only occurred for women in a few particular orders, including the Catalonian Order of the Hatchet or the Italian Order of the Glorious Saint Mary. The Order of the Hatchet was established to honor the women who defended the town of Tortosa in a battle. The men considered surrendering, "which the Women hearing of, to prevent the disaster threatening their City, themselves, and Children, put on men's Clothes, and by a resolute sally, forced the Moors to raise the Siege."[7] The dames admitted to the order received many privileges, including inheritance of their husbands' wealth in their own right, exemption from all taxes, and precedence over men in public assemblies. In England, 68 ladies were appointed to the Order of the Garter

7. Ashmole, Elias. The Institutions, Laws, & Ceremonies of the Most Noble Order of the Garter (London, by J. Macock, for Nathanael Brooke, 1672), Ch. 3, sect. 3.

between 1358 and 1488, while the Low Countries had a few orders exclusively open to noble women.[8]

PRIMOGENITURE

It's been made clear that brothers inherit before sisters; however, Westerosi law goes further than that. In Westeros, women have been prohibited from ruling the Seven Kingdoms in their own right since the Dance of the Dragons, a disastrous civil war that killed many of the Targaryens and their mythic mounts. In fact, the conflict began as a Targaryen princess, her father's firstborn, and his son by his second marriage both claimed the crown. Certainly, Daenerys is in denial about this law, though if she invades with enough troops and near-legendary dragons, the people of Westeros may crown her in any case.

The Dance of the Dragons mirrors an English war fought two generations after the Norman Conquest. King Henry I had all his nobles swear fealty to his daughter Mathilda. However, the widowed and childless Empress Mathilda had been sent off as a child bride to King Heinrich V of Germany and was a German-speaking stranger to her birth country and its customs. Likewise, Daenerys may consider herself a child of

8. H. E. Cardinale, Orders of Knighthood, Awards and the Holy See (UK: Van Duren, 1983), 214-215.

Westeros, but in fact, she's never lived there, only imagined it distantly. She may be in for a great surprise.

A few generations prior, the son of the English king had not inherited, but rather, the Saxon nobles voted for the most able male leader. With this recent history in place, and Mathilda far from the seat of power, King Henry's nephew Stephen rode hard for Winchester, where he seized the treasury, gathered support, and persuaded his brother, Bishop Henry of Winchester, to crown him King of England. Once he had been crowned, in the people's eyes he was king. Like charming, popular Renly, this king had an older brother, but ignored him, determined to claim the crown for himself.

Mathilda fought Stephen in a series of battles and won over the bishop's support at last. However, upon her triumph, her people began calling her "haughty" and "willful," complaining that she was acting like a female king—something her subjects weren't prepared to accept. As Helen Castor notes in her history book, *She-Wolves: The Women Who Ruled England before Elizabeth,* "The risk these queens ran was that their power would be perceived as a perversion of 'good' womanhood, a distillation of all that was to be feared in the unstable depths of female nature."[9]

In historical England, the first reigning queens,

9. Castor, She-Wolves 31.

Mary and Elizabeth, only appeared in the renaissance. Just before them, Henry VIII and Edward VI were respectively too incapacitated and too young to fight in battle, paving the way for "the humanist prince, entering the fray on the intellectual rather than the military front line" and thus preparing the country for female sovereigns.[10] Joffrey is expected to lead his battles himself, as Robb Stark and Stannis Baratheon do. Daenerys, of course, has proved equal to the challenge, riding her Silver across the sea. But will that be enough?

Empress Mathilda was finally forced to give the throne over to her teenage son Henry, who as Henry II always appreciated her council, even going so far as to call himself "Henry FitzEmpress."[11] Though she won her war, the English people were unwilling to give her the crown. Will this be Daenerys's fate, winning the throne but losing the popular vote due to her gender? Will she wed and give the throne to her husband and son? Or will she demand the rule in her own right?

MOTHER KNOWS BEST

> I wanted to make a strong mother character. The portrayal of women in epic fantasy have been problematical for a long time. These books are

10. Ibid., 28.
11. Ibid., 127.

> largely written by men but women also read them in great, great numbers. [...] Nobody wants to hear about King Arthur's mother and what she thought or what she was doing, so they get her off the stage and I wanted it too. And that's Catelyn.[12]

Thus Martin describes his desire to create Catelyn, the fighting mother of the saga. Martin adds:

> With Catelyn there is something reset for the Eleanor of Aquitaine, the figure of the woman who accepted her role and functions with a narrow society and, nonetheless, achieves considerable influence and power and authority despite accepting the risks and limitations of this society. She is also a mother.[13]

After her last child was born, and her mother-in-law Empress Mathilda had died, Eleanor of Aquitaine entered politics. At age forty-four, she introduced her teenage son Richard (one day to be Richard the Lionheart, King of England) to her home duchy of Aquitaine and crowned him as heir to her lands (Richard's older brother was her husband's heir). There she issued decrees, technically in Richard's name. Likewise, Catelyn Stark forges alliances for Robb in the Riverlands, where she grew up, trading on the people's personal loyalty to her.

Eventually, Queen Eleanor grew sick of her

12. "A Very Long Interview with George R.R. Martin."
13. Ibid.

husband King Henry II's decrees and raised three of her sons in rebellion against him. When she failed, her husband locked her away for fifteen years. Upon the king's death in 1189, Richard the Lionheart took the throne and released his mother, issuing the unprecedented decree that she might have "the power of doing whatever she wished in the kingdom" and making her a co-regent to himself.[14]

When Richard went on crusade, he was held for ransom in Austria, a capture instigated by his rebellious brother Prince John and King Philippe of France. The latter was the offended half-brother of Richard's former betrothed, Princess Alys. When, like Robb Stark, Richard broke his word while on campaign and married another, Philippe swore revenge. (Robb had better watch for the angered Freys.) Queen Eleanor delivered the ransom, amidst "anxious and difficult" negotiations.[15] As she had many adventures, riding to Jerusalem and leading her own troops in the Crusades, she made it clear that she was no traditional lady.

Medieval chroniclers insisted that a lady's place was in the castle, assisting her husband in his rule. However, such ladies were permitted and even encouraged to take arms to defend their lands on behalf of an underaged son or incapacitated

14. Ralph of Diceto qtd. in Castor, She-Wolves 195.
15. Eleanor of Aquitaine, qtd in Castor, She-Wolves 209.

husband. Catelyn Stark rousing her bannermen and leading them off to battle, or negotiating on her son's behalf, would not have been a great surprise in medieval Europe.

In 1342, Jeanne of Flanders, Countess of Montfort, fought in the names of her captured husband and young son. Chronicles of the time describe her admiringly:

> The countess of Montfort was there in full armour, mounted on a swift horse and riding through the town, street by street, urging the people to defend the town well. She made the women of the town, ladies and others, dismantle the carriageways and carry the stones to the battlements for throwing at their enemies. And she had bombards and pots full of quick lime brought to keep the enemy busy.[16]

She was not a knight, but a proper lady defending her homeland.

Lady Mormont of Bear Island and her many daughters do the same, in full armor and brandishing arms—her brother is commanding the Wall, and her nephew has fled to the east—she and her girls are the only Mormonts remaining, irrespective of gender.

Christine de Pizan insists a proper lady requires knowledge of law, accounting, warfare, agriculture, and textile production, adding:

16. Jean Froissart, Chroniques: Livre I, Le manuscrit d'Amiens, Bibliothèque municipale no. 486, ed. George T. Diller, trans. Helen Nicholson (1999). http://freespace.virgin.net/nigel.nicholson/wom5.htm.

> The lady who lives on her estates must be wise and must have the courage of a man...She must know the laws of warfare so that she can command her men and defend her lands if they are attacked.[17]

PIRATE QUEEN

Asha Greyjoy (called Yara on the show to avoid confusion with the wildling Osha) is a pirate captain, commanding thirty longships and conquering the Northern castle of Deepwood Motte. Of course, back home she's the lady of the Iron Islands, possibly her father's heir (though Ironmen expect a male lord so her position is precarious).

Historically, other female landowners led armies on the sea. Jeanne de Clisson, the "Lioness of Brittany" bought three warships, called the Black Fleet. (Yara's own ship is the Black Wind.) From 1343 to 1356, she harried the ships of King Philip VI. Likewise, the Irish "Pirate Queen" Grace O'Malley was another landowner-pirate, leading raids on the enemy English. She led hundreds of men in her fleet and proved herself "a master mariner, a brilliant strategist, and, above all, successful." Throughout her career Grace called the type of piracy she practiced "maintenance by land and sea," a type of protection racket.[18] While

17. Christine de Pizan, Le Livre des Trois Vertus, qtd in Bornstein, Diane. The Lady in the Tower: Medieval Courtesy Literature for Women. Hamden, Connecticut; Archon Books, 1983. 106.)

sailors were reluctant to sail *with* women, they sailed *under* highborn ladies on multiple occasions, in another example of the women fighting on behalf of their homelands.

ARYA

Brienne and Maege are the only heirs of their households, like many fighting women in history—they are the only ones who can gather their soldiers and lead them to war. By contrast, Arya is not the last heir of her household or even a warleader on behalf of her family. In fact, her father candidly tells her she will be married off like Sansa. However, Arya's brother Jon gives her a sword and her father arranges for dueling lessons, both historical anachronisms. Likewise, Meera Reed has a brother, but she is the better warrior with a long bronze knife, old iron greathelm, and wicked frog spear. This is another unlikely scenario, though her dressing in boys' clothes for safety of travel (as Arya does) is more realistic. Both girls have indulgent fathers, as Brienne does, and both are free to choose a boy's path.

Arya learns dueling from Syrio Forel of Braavos, another anachronism. Of the few known female duelists, most only fought as curiosities and performers when the real age of dueling had

18. Judith Cook, Pirate Queen: The Life of Grace O'Malley, 1530-1603 (USA: Mercier Press Ltd, 2004), 35.

long passed. In the seventeenth and eighteenth centuries, several woman-on-woman duels were recorded, usually over a man. Doña Ana Lezama de Urinza and Doña Eustaquia de Sonza, **known as the Valiant Ladies of Potosí,** snuck out at night dressed as a pair of caballeros (knights) to engage in street duels.[19] Dona Catalina de Erauso of Spain likewise became a soldier of fortune in Peru, dueling with sword, knife, and pistol.[20] 18th Century duelists included Mademoiselle La Maupin, Mademoiselle de Guignes, Mademoiselle d'Aiguillon, Mademoiselle Leverrier, Lady Almeria Braddock, Mrs. Elphinstone, Comptesse de Polignac and Marquise de Nesle. But on the streets of medieval Venice (the inspiration for Braavos), only male duelists were seen. Their famed assassins, a counterpart of Martin's Faceless Men were likewise male.

Martin's characters range from anachronisms like Arya to the real fighting ladies who rode to battle or took to the seas. In history and in fantasy, political pawns sold in marriage often gained extraordinary power as the regents and rulers of their worlds, though always with a male figurehead. The question remains whether Daenerys can hold the Iron Throne.

19. Jessica Amanda Salmonson, The Encyclopedia of Amazons (New York: Paragon House, 1991), 258.

20. Ibid., 258.

PART 4.

CONCLUSION

The series is continuing, with season four of the show renewed and uncounted seasons to follow. Martin has promised the saga will be finished in two more books, *The Winds of Winter* and *A Dream of Spring*. In April 2013, Martin reported he was about a quarter of the way through *The Winds of Winter,* a few chapters of which he's read at conventions. Martin tells fans, "I have many many more pages to do, but I have some great stuff planned for it: a lot of blood and fire and death and devastation and ravens coming home to roost."[1] As he puts it, they'll be "Two BIG books. 1500 manuscript pages each – that's 3000 pages. I think I have a good shot. And you know, if I really get pressed, I've already established that red comet. I can just have it hit Westeros and wipe out all life."[2]

He adds that he knows the ending "in broad strokes," commenting, "I don't know every little twist and turn that will get me there, and I don't know the ending of every secondary character. But the ending and the main characters, yeah. And [*Game of Thrones* producers] David Benioff and Dan Weiss know some of that too, which the fans are very worried about in case I get hit by a truck."

1. Laura Prudom, "Game Of Thrones' Season 3: George R. R. Martin On Writing 'The Bear And The Maiden Fair' And 'The Winds Of Winter,'" Huffington Post, Mar 20 2013. http://www.huffingtonpost.com/2013/03/20/game-of-thrones-season-3-george-r-r-martin_n_2915069.html
2. "George R. R. Martin Webchat Transcript." Empire Magazine. http://www.empireonline.com/interviews/interview.asp?IID=1496

[3] In a panel on season three, Benioff and Weiss admitted that they know who ends up on the Iron Throne. "There'll be a few people sitting on it before the end," Martin teases.[4]

Of course, much more story is waiting to unfold on the show. Book three and thus seasons three and four contain, by Martin's count:

> Four weddings, *two* funerals, and a wake. Four trials as well. And three dragons, four bears, many mammoths, an unkindness of ravens, and a turtle of unusual size. More battles, swordfights, and deaths than I can count, but two births as well, just to remind us all that life goes on.[5]

There's much more adventure to come...

3. James Hibberd, "EW Interview: George R.R. Martin talks 'A Dance With Dragons,'" EW.com, July 12 2011. http://shelf-life.ew.com/2011/07/12/george-martin-talks-a-dance-with-dragons.
4. Prudom, "Game Of Thrones' Season 3."
5. Correspondence with Fans," The Citadel: So Spake Martin, June 3 2000. http://www.westeros.org/Citadel/SSM/Category/C91/P180.

ABOUT THE AUTHOR

Valerie Estelle Frankel has won a Dream Realm Award, an Indie Excellence Award, and a USA Book News National Best Book Award for her Henry Potty parodies. She's the author of many books on pop culture, including From Girl to Goddess: The Heroine's Journey in Myth and Legend, Doctor Who – The What, Where, and How, and Teaching with Harry Potter. She has several Game of Thrones books, including the prophecy guide Winter is Coming, the fan guide Winning the Game of Thrones, and now Women in Game of Thrones and Symbols of Game of Thrones as well. Once a lecturer at San Jose State University, she's a frequent speaker at conferences. Come explore her research at www.vefrankel.com.

A SONG OF ICE AND FIRE BIBLIOGRAPHY

A Song of Ice and Fire Novels

A Game of Thrones, Bantam Books, 1996

A Clash of Kings, Bantam Books, 1999

A Storm of Swords, Bantam Books, 2000

A Feast for Crows, Bantam Books, 2005

A Dance with Dragons, Bantam Books, 2011

The Winds of Winter, forthcoming/Bantam Books

A Dream of Spring, forthcoming/Bantam Books

A Song of Ice and Fire Short Stories

Dunk and Egg:

"The Hedge Knight" (1998) available in George R.R. Martin, *Dreamsongs: Volume I* (Bantam Books, 2012)

"The Sworn Sword" (2003) available in George R.R. Martin, *Dreamsongs: Volume II* (Bantam Books, 2012)

"The Mystery Knight" (2010) available in *Warriors,* edited by George R.R. Martin and Gardner Dozois. Tor Books, 2010.

"The She-Wolves of Winterfell" Planned for inclusion in

Dangerous Women, now delayed and instead intended for a forthcoming Dunk and Egg collection.

Other

"The Princess and the Queen," (novella about the Targaryen Civil War called "The Dance of the Dragons") *Dangerous Women*, edited by George R.R. Martin and Gardner Dozois. Tor Books, 2013.

A Song of Ice and Fire Adaptations

A Game of Thrones: The Graphic Novel Series by Daniel Abraham (Adapter), George R.R. Martin (Author) and Tommy Patterson (Illustrator). Bantam Books. Ongoing.

The World of Ice and Fire: The Official History of Westeros and The World of A Game of Thrones by George R.R. Martin, Elio Garcia, and, Linda Antonsson. Bantam Books, 2013

The Lands of Ice and Fire (Poster Map) George R.R. Martin 2012

Printed in Great Britain
by Amazon